D1505446

Praise for *Becoming a Better Boss*

"In a world of relentless change, one of the few sources of competitive advantage for companies is the quality of their management practices. Top executives are increasingly looking for ways to rethink their management processes and systems. In this book, Julian Birkinshaw suggests a complementary approach – to push responsibility for rethinking management down to individual managers, and to help them find better ways of doing their job on an individual basis, one person at a time. *Becoming a Better Boss* is a revolutionary approach to management because it starts from the view of the person being managed, not the one doing the managing."

Gary Hamel, best-selling author and management thinker

"We know the secret of long term success is more engaged employees. In this book Julian Birkinshaw shows *how* managers can do a much better job of fully engaging the people around them, so they can do their best work."

David MacLeod, author of The MacLeod Report to the UK Government, "Engaging for Success"

"Great companies are defined by the quality of their managers. At Roche, we expect our managers to take a genuine interest in their people, to empower and trust them, and to exhibit integrity, courage and passion. This may sound straightforward, but it's not – it takes real effort and commitment to do these things on a sustained basis. In *Becoming a Better Boss*, Julian Birkinshaw provides a clear roadmap for how we can all become great managers."

Jayson Dallas, General Manager, Roche UK

"Good leadership and management begins with good people management and it's never been more important given the increasing diversity of the workforce and the ways in which we work. Julian's book speaks to these challenges and is full of great case studies, models, and ideas about how to effectively manage and engage the workforce of today, and of the future, for leaders at all levels. As he has done so often on the topics of management, he is able to bring new perspectives and insights and deliver these in a highly readable and engaging way."

Peter Cheese, CEO, Chartered Institute of Personnel and Development

"Julian's new book is perhaps the world's first discourse that looks at management from the eyes of the employees. With this simple yet path-breaking thought Birkinshaw ends up providing a practical roadmap for individuals to function effectively within an organization no matter how archaic/dysfunctional its structures or management machinery is."

Vineet Nayar, Vice Chairman, HCL Technologies

"One of the hallmarks of a truly successful company is its ability to harness the talents and skills of its employees across the world. In this book, Julian Birkinshaw shows why so many companies struggle with this, and he offers practical advice to help managers at all levels be more effective at getting the most out of their people."

Ayman Asfari, CEO, Petrofac

BECOMING A BETTER BOSS

WHY GOOD MANAGEMENT IS SO DIFFICULT

JULIAN BIRKINSHAW

JB JOSSEY-BASS™
A Wiley Brand

This book is dedicated to all the bad bosses I have worked for.
I couldn't have written this book without your help.

CONTENTS

PREFACE

I never expected to write this book. As a researcher and consultant, I had always focused my attention on the "big" challenges of strategy and structure that large organizations grapple with, leaving others to work on individual-level issues, such as how to motivate, influence, or develop others. However, over the last five years I have found myself drawn increasingly towards the nitty-gritty, practical challenges of how individuals actually get things done in large, complex organizations. It has been an enjoyable and surprising transition in my outlook on the world.

This journey of discovery began in 2006 when I founded the Management Innovation Lab (MLab) at London Business School with my colleague, Gary Hamel. The MLab mission was to accelerate the evolution of management, and our intention was to work closely with companies to design and run a series of management experiments that would help create new management practices and processes.

The MLab had some successes – we facilitated some important initiatives in companies, we wrote up our insights and ideas in some influential publications, and we spoke about the importance of management innovation in events around the world. However, we weren't as successful as we would have liked to be, especially when it came to making change stick. On many occasions, we helped groups of mid-level managers design and implement management experiments: a new approach to innovation, a way of bringing customer experience into the workplace, an initiative for eliminating bureaucracy. Even though the experiments typically worked well, they rarely made it to the next step. Instead, the ideas were killed off by invisible forces of inertia.

It was an eye-opener for me to observe first-hand how little support these mid-level managers were getting for their management experiments. Many observers have said that companies should become better at trying out small-scale experiments, as a way of de-risking their change programs, but it turns out that these small-scale experiments don't actually make much of a difference: they overcome the corporate immune system's first line of defence, but there is typically a second and then a third line of defence as well.

This led me to realize that reinventing management isn't just about rethinking the "system" of management, that is, the structures and processes through which work transpires. It is also about rethinking the "role" of management – the way individuals behave in the workplace in order to get things done. We have all observed individuals working in large organizations who are able to rise above the rules and procedures and to get things done through the force of their conviction. We can see such individuals as outliers and we can endeavor to build a better system to help ordinary people achieve the same results or we can see these individuals as role models who are showing others how to deal with the inevitable limitations of large bureaucratic organizations.

So over the last three years, I switched my focus – at least in part – to exploring the role of the individual manager in large complex organizations. This led me to develop my thoughts further on what makes for a successful "intrapreneur" – thoughts that I had first pursued in my doctoral dissertation 17 years earlier. It also led me deeper into the relationship between the manager and the employee. Management, it is often said, is about getting the most out of your employees, so a good manager is someone who really understands what makes his or her people tick. Of course, the notion that managers need to see the world through the eyes of their employees is an old one, but I was still surprised how few of the current writers on management actually gave much attention to it. Most preferred to write about management from a rather elitist perspective – from the point of view of the person doing the managing, rather than the person being managed.

This new focus resulted in a report on "Employee Centred Management" that I published in 2011, with funding from HCL Technologies and help from my co-authors Lisa Duke, Vyla Rollins, and Stefano Turconi. This study included a lot of data from employees in large companies about their fears and motivations at work, and their manager's style of working. It also included materials from my research interviews and from my own "ethnographic" experiences of life working on the front line. I have now expanded on those findings and developed my ideas further, and this book is the result.

I see this as a complement to my previous book, *Reinventing Management*. If *Reinventing Management* was a roadmap to help you make better choices in the "architecture" of management in your organization, then *Becoming a Better Boss* is about helping you, as an individual, to function effectively. I wrote it particularly to help those managers who are frustrated by the lack of change in their organizations and who are seeking to make a real difference. However, the ideas are actually relevant to pretty much any manager, regardless of their level of ambition. *Becoming a Better Boss* is about understanding your employees, your organization, and yourself more acutely, and developing a way of working that treats these components as they are, rather than as you would like them to be.

ACKNOWLEDGMENTS

This book is the product of many conversations and interviews I have had over the last five years. I have talked to CEOs about these issues and I have talked to front-line employees with no management experience at all. I have also spent a great deal of time kicking my ideas round with colleagues and friends. Unlike some of my previous books on rather arcane subjects, this is one that everyone can relate to, so the people I have talked to are numerous. While I will do my best to acknowledge everyone who has helped me, I apologize in advance for those I have temporarily forgotten.

First I would like to thank London Business School, which provides the perfect blend of practical relevance and theoretical rigor for me to pursue a project of this type. Individuals at the School who have helped me include Andrew Likierman, Karen Napier, Lynda Gratton, Costas Markides, Jules Goddard, Holly Parker, Vyla Rollins, Rob James, Alan Matcham, Lisa Duke, and Stefano Turconi.

Gary Hamel continues to be a source of inspiration for all my work on management. Many of the ideas I developed in this book started from casual conversations with him. Gary's colleagues at the Management Innovation Exchange, Michele Zanini and Polly LaBarre, were also helpful for several of the stories in this book.

Simon Caulkin and Ngaire McKeown helped me to write some of the company case studies that I used in this book.

Many others have also provided useful insights and examples. In no particular order, these include Peter Cheese and John McGurk at CIPD; Tim Brooks at the *British Medical Journal*; David Smith formerly of Asda; Andrew Dyckhoff of Merrick; Vineet Nayar, Anand Pillai, Bindi Bhullar, and Ani Mukherjee at HCL Technologies; Stephen Martin at Clugston; Ross Smith at Microsoft; Andy Mulholland and Rick Mans at Capgemini; Chris Bayliss at National Australia Bank;

Jordan Cohen and Siri Uotila at PA Consulting; Stefan Arn and Christian Crowden at AdNovum; Paul Lambert, Jesper Ek, and Steffi Mitchell at Roche; Torgeir Jacobsen, Hakan Johansson, Niclas Ward, Jorgen Hiden, and Katarina Mohlin at If Insurance; Julie Powell at Rio Tinto; Paul Flaum, Lorena Dominguez, and Peter Gardiner at Premier Travel Inn.

I thank Wiley/Jossey-Bass for pulling the book together and helping me to sharpen up the key ideas, especially Rosemary Nixon, Nick Mannion, Kathe Sweeney, and Patricia Bateson.

Finally, thanks as always to my family, to Laura, Ross, Duncan, and Lisa, for putting up with my long hours of writing. I couldn't have done it without your support!

INTRODUCTION

One of the defining features of Google's management model – alongside it's fun working environment – is its analytical, data-driven approach to decision-making. New products are launched through carefully controlled experiments. Highly paid persons' opinions – HIPPOs for short – are disdained. The company's chief economist has even predicted that the sexy job in the next 10 years will be statisticians.

So it is no surprise that when Google started to review its management practices, in early 2009, it took a data-driven approach. Led by the VP for people operations, Laszlo Bock, and codenamed Project Oxygen, the initiative involved gathering more than 10 000 observations from performance reviews, feedback surveys, and interviews[1]. After a lot of number-crunching, as well as some subjective interpretation, the project team came up with a list of eight ranked factors that defined the really good managers at Google:

1. Be a good coach.

2. Empower your team and don't micromanage.

3. Express interest in team members' success and personal well-being.

4. Don't be a sissy: be productive and results-oriented.

5. Be a good communicator and listen to your team.

6. Help your employees with career development.

7. Have a clear vision and strategy for the team.

8. Have key technical skills so you can help advise the team.

This is a good list. We can all agree, I think, that these are desirable attributes for managers. It even includes a few surprises – technical skills had always been considered very important in Google's geeky, technocratic environment, yet they were ranked far lower than "softer" skills around coaching and empowering people. The analysis helped Google to think much more stringently about the types of people they wanted as department heads and team leaders.

But it is also a useless list. Why? Because we already knew all this. With the possible exception of "don't be a sissy," I have seen versions of this list in every book ever written on management. When I run seminars with executives or with MBA students, it takes about 20 minutes to construct this list simply by drawing out the experiences of those in the room. Adam Bryant, writing in *The New York Times*, called the list "forehead-slappingly obvious . . . reading like a white-board gag from an episode of The Office."

So here is the problem. Let's say you work at Google and you want to improve your managerial skills. Are you going to study this list and evaluate your progress against each of the eight points? Are you going to pin it up next to your desk, so you can refer to it next time you are meeting with one of your team? My guess is you are not. This list is about as useful to you in becoming a better manager as "ten steps to a healthier diet" to an overweight businessman or "how to perfect your golf swing" to an aspiring Rory McIlroy. In all these cases, we can read the words and we know what we are supposed to do. But we don't know where to start, we don't know how to prioritize among the list of points, and we don't know how to get out of our old habits. So our behavior remains unchanged.

This gap between what we "know" and what we "do" provides the primary motivation for this book. If we are to improve the practice of management, we need to move beyond how-to lists and engage in a more thoughtful inquiry about what we are trying to achieve and what the obstacles are that prevent us from achieving it. I wrote this book, in other words, to *help you become a better boss*, but don't expect any simple bullet-point lists of things to do. If being a good manager was as simple as following a list of instructions, anyone could do it!

BUILDING A BETTER BUSINESS

There is also a secondary motivation for this book, namely a concern for the overall success and welfare of large business organizations. As I write this in 2012, we face a very uncertain economic future. While the macroeconomic story is the one that gathers most of the headlines, I believe a lot of the problems of the last few years can be attributed to failures of management and leadership in our large companies.

The financial services sector has, not unreasonably, attracted most of the negative attention. Whether the offence is manipulating Libor, laundering money in Mexico, mis-selling pensions, or rogue trading, the cause is always some sort of underlying deficiency in governance or culture that makes the company in question prone to poor decision-making. But plenty of other sectors have also been fingered in the last couple of years – BP's oil spill was condemned as an "overarching failure of management," Rupert Murdoch's News Corporation was found to have "failed to exercise proper oversight" following the phone-hacking scandal, and pharmaceutical company GSK was fined $3 billion for unethical drug-selling practices[2].

In these and many other cases, bad management is indeed to blame. But it is not worth just pointing the finger at the CEO. Typically he takes the hit, as he should, but the problems of a deficient culture or governance system usually stem from decisions made many years earlier. In fact, I would argue that many of the management failures we are seeing today can be traced back to an "industrial era" model of management that is no longer fit for purpose. This model – with its emphasis on coordination through formal rules, hierarchical decision-making, and extrinsic rewards – worked well for many years, but is ill-suited to today's fast-paced, knowledge-based business world.

My previous book, *Reinventing Management*, focused on these big picture issues. It described how executives can challenge these deep-seated assumptions about how large organizations work and how they can devise new and better ways of working.

This book tackles the same problems from the other direction, that is, by focusing on the choices each of us makes, every day, about how we get our work done. The goal, essentially, is to reinvent the practice of management one person at a time. If each one of us becomes more effective in our managerial work, we don't just improve the working lives of those around us, we also become agents of change for this broader endeavour as well – to build better businesses.

THE WAY FORWARD

The central idea in this book is that we can all become better bosses by starting with a more realistic set of assumptions about the challenges we face in the workplace. There are three problems with the standard advice that is offered.

First, it is usually offered *from the perspective of the person doing the managing*. Most management books and articles are written by successful executives looking back on their careers, or by academics or consultants who have interviewed or advised these same executives. We get a view of how these individuals think and how they achieved what they did. But it is an incomplete story, because it doesn't give a voice to the people being managed – the employees through whom the manager achieved his or her objectives.

Second, it starts from *a very rational view of human nature*. Google is a company of engineers where data is king. So not surprisingly, their approach to improving management in the company is to see what the data says and to codify the results of their analysis in a way that everyone can understand. Google is hardly alone in this – most large companies have carefully developed lists of management "competencies" and most books on management have recipe books for aspiring managers to follow. But this rational perspective is a gross simplification of reality. There is now a great deal of evidence that we often behave in an unpredictable and nonrational manner, and often in ways we don't even realize.

Third, it assumes that the work of management is happening *within a reasonably sensible organizational environment*, where objectives are clear, decisions are implemented, and rules are followed. Again, though, we know that many organizations are not remotely reasonable or sensible. People pursue their own pet objectives, they subvert decisions, and they bend the rules. Managers often end up succeeding despite the system, not because of it.

Given all these realities, is it a surprise that the standard advice goes unheeded? Or fails to make a lasting impression on the way we work?

In this book I put forward a perspective on management that starts from a very different set of assumptions.

First, and most importantly, I take an employee's eye-view of management. I focus on the needs, motivations, and fears of those working on the front lines of their companies, and ask them what they are looking for in their managers. I examine cases where managers have completely misunderstood the needs of their employees, and have paid the price, as well as cases where they have done an exemplary job of seeing the world through the eyes of those doing the work. This perspective suggests some important new techniques for becoming more attentive and helping our employees to do their best work.

Second, I encourage you to look in the mirror and to confront the biases and frailties that are preventing you from being a really good manager. I show that, for most of us, being a good manager is an "unnatural act" – something that we can learn to do, but only with a lot of deliberate effort. By understanding the three primary areas of tension between our subconscious instinct and our rational mind, we can become more effective at making the right choices when it really matters.

Third, I rethink the role of the individual manager when the organization he or she works for is dysfunctional. I describe the typical pathologies and limitations of large companies and some of the coping strategies that managers use to get things done despite the structure. I also introduce the notion of active experimentation – the idea that you can make conscious but low-risk changes to the way work gets done within your own part of the company.

These three perspectives are summarized below and they provide the overall structure for the book.

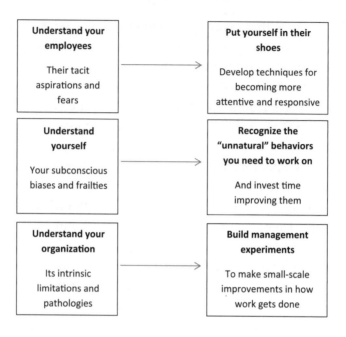

WHO IS THE BOOK FOR?

As you should have gathered by now, there are no "silver bullets" for becoming a better boss; no hard-and-fast rules for improving the practice of management. So I am not going to fall into the trap of providing you with a how-to list that summarizes all these ideas. Good management has an analytical component – the folks in Google aren't crazy – but it is mostly about building deep expertise in relating to other people. Like improving our golf swing, we become better managers through practice, feedback, and reflection. And like trying to lose weight, we become more effective when we have got to grips with our own biases and frailties as human beings. So while there are no silver bullets, there are plenty of little tricks we can play on ourselves, and plenty of exercises we can try that will help us develop the expertise we need to succeed.

I have three types of reader in mind for this book:

- You as a manager of others. The book is all about the things you can do differently – to give you a new outlook on your work, to help you reflect on your own biases, and to force yourself out of your comfort zone.

- You as an employee. This book will help you understand why your manager isn't as helpful, articulate, or forgiving as you think he or she should be. And it will also help you to manage him or her more effectively. It is sometimes said that you get the manager you deserve: I don't entirely buy that, but I do believe you have some degree of freedom to help your manager do the job better.

- You as a manager of other managers. Many of the obstacles to good management discussed in this book are not set in stone. If you want your own people to become more effective in their work, there are plenty of things you can do to facilitate their improvement.

The book is in two main parts. The first part provides the motivation and background for the core ideas in the book. I show how important it is to take management seriously (Chapter 1), I sketch out the key dimensions of management and where it usually goes wrong (Chapter 2), and I take a deep dive into the worldview of the employee (Chapter 3).

The second part provides a detailed discussion of the three alternative perspectives: a re-interpretation of management through the eyes of the employee (Chapter 4), an exploration of our own biases and frailties and how we can overcome them (Chapter 5), and a discussion of the use of active experimentation to overcome the limitations and pathologies of the organizations we work for (Chapter 6).

The final chapter (Chapter 7) looks to the future, to make sense of how technology and other forces are changing the practice of management. Taken as a whole, the flow of the book represents an arc, from the "big picture" concerns addressed in Chapter 1, down to the worldview of the employee and manager, and then back up to the big picture again.

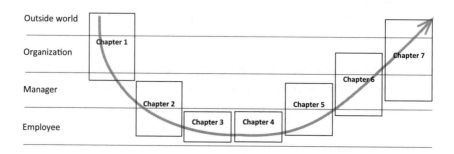

— 1 —

WHY MANAGEMENT MATTERS

One of the motivations in writing this book was to tackle the following puzzle:

- Do we know how to generate sustainably high performance in companies? Yes we do.

- Do companies consistently follow this established formula? No they don't.

On the face of it, this seems strange. Surely human nature compels us to seek out better ways of doing things? Surely competition between companies creates a survival-of-the-fittest push for constant improvement? Well, yes it does, but there are also many other forces at work that can frustrate our ability to do what we know to be right. Sometimes these forces prevail, leaving everyone stuck with an inferior model.

The established "formula" for delivering high performance is what I call a people-centric approach to management. It involves hiring talented and motivated people, providing them with the competencies they need to succeed, and – most important of all – putting in place a system of management that enables them to do their best work.

Do you buy the argument that a people-centric approach to management is key to long-term success? When I ask this question in seminars, the majority of people say yes: they intuitively buy the argument. However, when I probe further, it becomes clear that a significant number are more sceptical – they aren't *convinced* its true, but they figure that investing in people doesn't do much harm and perhaps it is just one of the costs of being in business, so they go along with it. Then there are the cynics, usually a fairly small number of people, who strongly disagree – they think this emphasis on people is misguided or insincere, or perhaps even a Machiavellian way for managers to further their own objectives.

I will get back to the views of the cynics later, in Chapter 3, but for now, I want to concentrate on those in the first two groups. I was in the first category when I started researching this book. I saw the link between investing in people and corporate performance as axiomatic – self-evidently true, but so fundamental that it probably couldn't be proved.

DRIVERS OF CORPORATE PERFORMANCE

It turns out I was half-right. When you collect the evidence together, it shows that the axiom is not only correct but is also objectively verifiable. Several recent academic studies have shown that companies with engaged and happy employees outperform those that do not[1]. There has also been a lot of applied research in recent years, such as the "Engage for Success" movement in the UK, which has drawn similar conclusions[2].

One particular study is worth recounting here in detail. A London Business School Professor, Alex Edmans, studied the "Best Companies to Work For" in the United States and focused on their stock market performance over a 25 year period. He showed that "A value-weighted portfolio of the 100 Best Companies earned an annual alpha of 3.5% from 1984 to 2009." In plain English, this means that if you invested your own pension in these companies, and left it there, you would get a significantly better return – 3.5% per year – than the average fund manager[3]. Edmans showed, in other words, that not only do these "Best Companies to Work For" have better performance over the long-term than those in the market as a whole but also the stock market fails to pick up on their superior prospects.

Remember, stock markets are supposed to be efficient. If Apple announces a new category-busting product or if Roche gets a patent on a new cancer drug, their shares rise in anticipation of future growth. However, when *Fortune* magazine announces the annual list of winners in the Best Companies to Work For ranking, the stock market doesn't care. This information just doesn't make it on to the analysts' radar screens. Implicitly, investors seem to be saying, "OK, so you take care of your employees well, good for you; but we won't be buying up your shares until we have seen how that investment works its way through to the bottom line."

To say this even more simply, analysts and professional investors don't buy this "soft stuff." Even with solid evidence that investing in people makes a long-term difference to performance, they retain their sceptical position. As one analyst said, "Costco's management is focused on . . . employees to the detriment of shareholders. To me, why would I want to buy a stock like that?[4]"

So why the scepticism? To answer this question, it is useful to go back to economic theory because stock markets are heavily influenced by that body of thinking. For many economists, employees are still nothing more than an input cost. Companies invest in workers in the same way they invest in plant and machinery and technology; they spend as little as they can, they sell their product for as much as they can, and the difference is profit. If this is true, then spending more than you have to on employees is just throwing money away. Of course, this is a gross simplification, and indeed there are many alternative economic theories that recognize the unusual nature of human capital, but old theories die hard, and the aggregate view is still one that treats "intangible assets" like expertise and discretionary effort with suspicion.

Perhaps this is starting to change. An extensive research program led by Professors John van Reenen (London School of Economics) and Nick Bloom (Stanford) over the last decade has sought to shed light on why we see big productivity differences between seemingly similar companies. They show that quality of management is the key – some companies simply use better management practices, in a more consistent way, than others and these practices have a significant impact on productivity and performance. This isn't a surprising finding to those who work in or study the field of management, but it is helping to shape the conversation among economists about how companies *really* work.

Regardless of what investors and analysts think, the key point is that there is a well-established formula for achieving long-term corporate success, and it is about investing in people and fostering a high level of employee engagement. To be clear, these effects are true in aggregate, but not in every specific case, and there are many other drivers of corporate success as well. But these are small caveats; the overall body of evidence is still sufficiently strong to make investing in people a smart strategy for your company, and investing in people-centric companies a smart strategy for your pension.

QUALITY OF LIFE CONSIDERATIONS

So much for the investor or owner's perspective. What about the broader view? How does a people-centric approach to business affect society as a whole? The evidence here is equally persuasive. There have been many research studies showing, for example, that engaged employees have lower levels of absenteeism, high levels of overall well-being, and even lower incidences of disease[5]. Moreover, the principle of employee well-being is as old as the field of management itself. Students of business history are familiar with the concept of *Corporate Welfarism* from the 1880s[6] and the *Quality of Work Life* movement in the 1950s.

Today, there is currently a huge amount of interest in happiness and positive psychology. Studies have ranked countries by how happy their people are (top of the list: Denmark)[7]. Policy-makers have put programs in place to foster more positive attitudes at work and home. In the UK, Prime Minister David Cameron has picked up on this trend, by launching an initiative to start measuring National Well-being alongside traditional economic measures such as GDP. He said we need to "start measuring our progress as a country not just by how our economy is growing, but by how our lives are improving; not just by our standard of living, but by our quality of life.[8]" (for more information on this initiative, see the website www.engageforsuccess.org).

Of course there are many factors that shape our quality of life and the world of work only represents one part of the story. But for those of us in full-time employment, the quality of our working lives has a huge impact on our overall well-being and indirectly on the well-being of our families. Think of it from the employer's perspective. If your employees spend 40–50 hours a week in the office, you owe it to them to make it as worthwhile and pleasant as possible – not just because that is morally the right thing to do but also because happy employees are healthier and more productive.

Again, the evidence suggests that a people-centric model in the corporate world isn't just good for performance; it is also good for the people working in that company and society as a whole. Now, I realize that this sort of "win-win" story makes people a bit suspicious: surely there is a catch? Surely there is, at least, an opportunity cost to this sort of investment?

Well, there might be, but the truth is, we don't know. The reason we don't know is that despite all the evidence that this people-centric approach is better, there are actually remarkably few companies that have implemented it on a consistent basis.

THE RHETORIC–REALITY GAP

Greg Smith caused quite a stir in March 2012 when he wrote a scathing op-ed in *The New York Times*, "Why I am leaving Goldman Sachs.[9]" He said the company was morally bankrupt and that its culture of teamwork, integrity, and humility had been lost.

I don't have the inside story on what Goldman is really like, but Greg Smith's description sounds remarkably like every other investment bank on Wall Street or in the City of London. It is the oldest story in the book: when big bonuses are on the line, people become greedy, they look out for their own interests, and collaboration, integrity, and humility go out the window. The culture in these banks is individualistic and aggressive. Bad management is tolerated. People are expendable.

Whether accurate or not, my point here is a simple one, namely that *the world Greg Smith described in his New York Times article was exactly the opposite of what Goldman Sachs says about itself.* The company website says, "Our people are our greatest asset. We say it often and with good reason . . . at every step of our employees' careers we invest in them. . . our goal is to maximize individual potential."

So if we want to get a fix on how people-centric companies really are, we can start by entirely disregarding any public statements they might make. A much better approach is to ask employees, preferably in an anonymous way, about how happy or engaged they are, or how good their managers are. It is also useful to gather objective data about, for example, levels of employee turnover or cases of harassment and bullying. Once you get this sort of information, the story that emerges is not a happy one. Here are some examples of recent studies:

- Human resource consultancy Towers Perrin (now Towers Watson) measures employee engagement levels across countries and sectors. On an aggregate level, its 2003 data showed that 17% of the sample were highly engaged, 64% were moderately engaged, and 19% were disengaged with their work.

- A poll of workers in the UK commissioned by the Trade Unions Congress (TUC) in 2008 found that only 43% of employees were fully engaged in the work they were doing[10].

- The UK's Chartered Institute of Personnel Development (CIPD) does a quarterly "employee outlook" survey. In July 2012, they found that only 38% of employees were actively engaged at work, with 59% neutral, and 3% disengaged. While respondents felt their managers mostly treated them fairly (71%), less than half were satisfied with the level of coaching and feedback they received[11].

The picture that emerges from these and other studies is pretty clear. There are some very well-managed companies out there with highly motivated and engaged employees. There are also some dire companies with miserable employees who are investing more time looking for a new job than doing the work they are paid more. The vast majority of companies are stuck in the middle, no doubt trying hard to improve their people-management practices but without the buy-in they need to make it a real priority and without the results to show for it. Such companies typically have pockets of excellence, but a great deal of mediocrity as well.

There is, in short, a rhetoric–reality gap between the words and policies of top executives and the experiences of front-line employees. Figure 1.1 provides an illustration of this gap, from some research I was involved with[12]: it shows employees answer the same questions less positively the lower you go in the corporate hierarchy.

This gap causes problems in a couple of ways. First, it creates confusion: when employees see a disconnect between the stated priorities of the company and the decisions that are enacted on a day-to-day basis, they don't know where to focus their efforts. Second, it breeds

Figure 1.1 The Rhetoric–Reality Gap: employees have very different views on corporate practices, depending on where they sit in the company

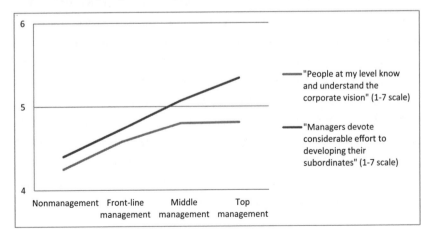

cynicism: an underlying sense that top executives are out of touch and therefore not to be fully trusted.

The presence of this large rhetoric–reality gap opens up a couple of important questions. First, why is the gap so large? If the evidence favoring a people-centric approach to management is so strong, why don't companies actually do what they know they should? Second, what can we do to close this gap? What steps can we take – as individuals and as management teams – to make a real difference to the way our companies are managed? In the remainder of this chapter, and in Chapter 2, I will suggest a way we might tackle this first question. The second question then motivates the remainder of the book.

EXPLAINING THE PUZZLE

Let's return to the puzzle I introduced at the beginning of this chapter. If a proven better model exists, wouldn't we expect people to gravitate towards it? Well, yes we would, but it doesn't always work out that way. Sometimes an inferior model wins out and sometimes the better model never takes off.

Consider that old favorite, the battle for supremacy in the personal computer industry. Apple's operating system and user interface were vastly superior to anything IBM or Microsoft had to offer in the early 1980s, and even today most people would still agree that Apple's operating system and user interface are second-to-none. However, Apple's worldwide market share in the PC/laptop industry is stuck at around 5–10%, well below that of leaders like HP, Dell and Lenovo.

Another classic story, though from a completely different context, is a study reported by Everett Rogers in his book *The Diffusion of Innovations*. Health workers in Peru were trying to persuade villagers to boil their water to reduce illness, but these villagers didn't understand the science behind boiling water, they were sceptical of outsiders telling them to change their ways, and boiling water was stigmatized as something only unwell people would do. The two-year campaign was considered largely unsuccessful.

Under certain circumstances, then, the better way of doing things doesn't take off. Sometimes, as in the Apple–Microsoft case, the problem is simply that we get locked into a suboptimal way of working and the costs of changing (throwing out our Windows PC, learning how to use the new software) outweigh the potential benefits (a slightly better user experience). At other times, and the Peruvian villagers illustrate this nicely, the problem is a lack of buy-in to the new way of working: lack of understanding of the potential benefits, distrust of the people selling it to us, and concerns about how risky or expensive it will be to implement.

These examples help to shed light on why we don't see widespread adoption of the proven people-centric model in the corporate world. As with the PC industry, companies are "locked" into an old model of management that views employees as input factors and they are saddled with traditional beliefs and processes that reinforce that view. As with the Peruvian villager story, companies are suspicious of the "better" model that involves investing in and empowering people. They are sceptical of the outsiders – the consultants and academics – pushing the new model and they aren't convinced that it will work for them.

WHY COMPANIES STRUGGLE TO CHANGE

To test out these ideas, some colleagues and I conducted a survey, asking managers from around the world for their views on the future of management[13]. First, we asked where the biggest gaps were – between how important a set of managerial challenges were and the amount of progress their companies had made. The biggest gaps were in how we make sense of our world and relate to each other: the need to *Retrain Managerial Minds, Further Unleash Human Imagination, Depoliticize Decision Making*, and *Reduce Fear, Increase Trust* (see Box 1.1: The Biggest Challenges in Management). So no real surprises there – our respondents told us, in essence, that it is difficult to fully make sense of and buy into this new way of working.

BOX 1.1 THE BIGGEST CHALLENGES IN MANAGEMENT

We asked respondents to rank a series of "moonshots" in terms of the importance that their organization makes progress on them (where 1 = unimportant, 2 = important, 3 = essential). We also asked respondents to evaluate the amount of progress their organization had already made on each challenge (1 = little, 2 = modest, 3 = substantial). By calculating the difference between the two scores (importance less progress made), we were able to draw up a list of the most critical challenges facing management today. These are the areas where the biggest opportunity for management innovation exists. The top five were as follows:

Retrain managerial minds. In today's creative economy, deductive and analytical skills are table stakes. What makes a difference for wealth creation is creative skills – the ability to conceptualize, to "think outside the box," to take a system-wide view of a problem. The trouble is, many companies don't truly value these skills and most don't have the first idea how to evaluate or develop them. This is why retraining managerial minds came out first in the survey – there is a yawning gap between rhetoric and reality here.

Further unleash human imagination. This is almost a subset of the first point. If we need to retrain managerial minds, perhaps the biggest deficit is the lack of human imagination in the workplace. It is no secret that traditional organization structures suppress imagination and creativity. What is surprising is how little progress we seem to have made, despite our acute awareness of the problem. Perhaps we need to look to nonbusiness organizations, from theatre groups to NGOs, for inspiration in how to train and make the most of really creative people.

Depoliticize decision-making. Max Weber, the German sociologist, saw bureaucracy as the antidote to corporate politics. He envisioned decisions being made according to formal rules rather than the whim of an autocratic leader. But bureaucracy failed us, and we ended up creating organizations that allowed, and perhaps even encouraged, individuals at all levels to pursue their personal agendas and to abrogate responsibility for the outcomes of their actions. There are known remedies, such as direct democracy, opinion markets, and online voting systems that can be readily applied. However, it's surprising how few of these remedies are actually used on a consistent basis.

Develop holistic performance measures. Performance measurement tools have improved considerably over the last few decades, but they still suffer from a bias towards quantifiable, short-term metrics, and towards the needs of shareholders. The challenge here is to build systems that embrace a broader set of stakeholders needs and that don't rely on narrow quantitative measures. How can we measure the true impact of our activities on the communities we touch and the world we operate in? What would a balanced scorecard incorporating the needs of our grandchildren look like? Few companies have given much attention to these questions.

Reduce fear, increase trust. Half a century on, Deming's imperative that we take fear out of the workplace is as salient as ever. Many employees, even in well-run organizations, work with a nagging sense of fear that dampens their initiative and pushes them towards mediocrity. We all know what is needed is a trusting culture – one in which new ideas are supported and well-intentioned failures are celebrated – but the gap between knowing and doing in this area is enormous.

Why did these five come out on top? Because employees can relate to them at a very personal level. Fear and trust are sensations we feel on a daily basis; we experience the fallout from politically motivated decisions directly and most of us have plenty of latent creativity and passion that doesn't find an outlet in the workplace. The odd one out was the perceived need for holistic performance measures, which was perhaps shaped by our desire to make sense of the financial crisis (the survey was conducted in 2009).

The second part of the survey asked respondents what the biggest barriers to change were. In other words, we were asking them why the rhetoric–reality gap existed. After grouping their answers into categories, we ended up with the following as the biggest barriers:

- Limited bandwidth: not enough time, too few resources (19% of all responses)
- Old and orthodox thinking (15%)
- Disincentives to act: fear of change, executive self-interest (14%)

How do we interpret these answers? In my view, the managers in the survey were saying: we would love to pursue these exciting challenges, but we are already running at full pace, with no slack; our colleagues and our bosses have no interest in disrupting the status quo; and we are so stuck in old-style thinking that we cannot imagine an alternative. It is almost a cry for help.

Going back to the Apple–Microsoft analogy, they are saying that they are locked into a badly wired operating system. They would love to move out of it, and into a better system, but the switching costs are too high. So while there may be some problems of a lack of *understanding* of the better alternatives out there, the bigger problem appears to be a lack of *capability* to make the necessary changes.

When I speak on these issues, I often get the audience – typically mid/senior executives in large companies – to offer their views. Why, I ask, is the world of management stuck with an inferior model when we have such solid evidence that there are better ways of working out there? The audience typically echoes many of the points noted above, but they also bring some additional insights.

The first is that a people-centric approach to management is *systemic*. You can't just train people in new ways of working, or measure their performance differently, or change the reward system, or hire on attitude rather than skill, or change the promotion criteria: you have to do all these things. Each one reinforces the other, and so it is only by creating the "bundle" of people-centric systems that you get the improvement in performance that is being sought[14].

The second is that a people-centric approach to management is a *long-term investment*. Behavior change takes time, so even if all the necessary changes are put in place, the desired performance improvement is likely to kick in several years later. For many executives, a 4–5 year return on investment is simply too slow to be worth doing – they know they will have moved on to their next challenge before the results are through.

Finally, the people-centric approach to management is *fragile*. It assumes people are competent and committed to the company's goals and it gives them a lot of discretion in how they act. But it only works if everyone plays along. For example, you might want to give your team a lot of space to experiment with new ways of working, but that only works if your boss is also prepared to give *you* the freedom to fail. Or consider the case of a single rogue trader who cheats the system: he loses his job, but everyone also suffers because the rules get tightened up company-wide to avoid the same thing happening again.

In fact, the more you think about it, the easier it is to understand why we have made so little progress towards this demonstrably better people-centric model of management. The inertial forces in our complex organizations are very strong and it seems that no amount of effort can fully overcome them.

Surely some progress has been made? What about, for example, the "Best Companies to Work For" that were mentioned at the beginning of the chapter? Yes, indeed. So, as we look at the entire organizational landscape, there are certainly companies that have implemented various forms of people-centric management. Indeed, without such cases we wouldn't be able to say that a proven better model exists. A closer look at these "outlier" cases is instructive. They can be put into three groups:

1. Small and/or relatively young companies with impressive and often quirky people-centric models. Examples include the software companies Red Gate (UK), Red Hat (US), and AdNovum (Switzerland); training company Happy Ltd (UK); recruitment consultancy Twenty (UK), and consultants Brand Velocity (US) and Nixon McInnes (UK).

2. Established companies that have always had a people-centric approach and are still heavily influenced by their founders. Examples include WL Gore, Whole Foods Market, SAS Institute, South West Airlines, Google, Amazon, and John Lewis.

3. Large established companies that are working very hard to reinvent themselves using these alternative principles. Examples include HCL Technologies, Standard Chartered Bank, and Procter & Gamble.

The trouble with this list is the following. Most of Group 1 will end up gravitating towards the traditional model of management as they grow, because it is safe, established, and predictable. Some will end up as Group 2 companies, but these are hard to learn from, because they have always operated with their unusual model. They are also susceptible to losing their distinctiveness, especially when there is a change in leadership or their ownership model changes (e.g., through a stock-market listing). Group 3 companies, while impressive, are few in number and always at risk of being sucked back towards the traditional model.

To summarize the argument so far: there is a proven "better way" of managing, one that involves putting people first and creating an environment in which they can do their best work. However, very few companies have implemented it because it is difficult to do, requires long-term investment, and makes investors nervous.

How you interpret this statement depends on your outlook on life. If you are a pessimist, you will focus on the barriers to change and the lock-in problem, and you will likely conclude that this people-centric model will never take off. If you are an optimist, you will point to the list of outliers, the companies that have lit up the way forward, and you will conclude that we are on the cusp of dramatic improvements in the way companies are managed.

I am a pragmatist: I think fundamental improvements in management are possible, but I expect progress to be slow and that it won't happen without strong leadership. I have spent a lot of time over the last five years working with companies on this exact challenge. I know how difficult it is to make positive and lasting changes in how companies are run. But I have also seen glimpses of success, and certainly enough to make the effort worthwhile.

WHY INDIVIDUAL MANAGERS STRUGGLE TO CHANGE

This chapter has focused on the company as a system: a community of individuals working together through established rules and procedures to achieve a common objective. I have argued that this system is often so complex, and its elements so tightly interwoven, that it becomes inert, even in the face of compelling evidence that it should change.

However, we can also pursue a similar line of argument at the individual level. If our bureaucratic management systems help perpetuate a broken model of management, perhaps our own individual beliefs, motivations, and interests are also playing their part?

Here are a few simple questions to get you thinking. Do you invest your time in things that help others to succeed? Do you invest in projects that will help the company in the long run, even if you won't be around to get any credit for their success? Are you prepared to try out a new way of working that may fail, even if you risk looking foolish?

Most people would like to answer yes to these questions – but the evidence says that most of us actually do these things pretty rarely. For the most part, we prefer to invest in things that help us meet our own goals, provide short-term success, and with as little risk as possible. This, in a nutshell, is the real reason why change is so hard in companies. Good management goes against many of our natural predispositions as individuals, and as a result we often behave in ways that make progress difficult.

If we want enduring change in how companies work, we need to tackle the problem from both sides: we need to rethink the "architecture" of management to engage and motivate individual employees, but we also need to rethink the "practice" of management, one person at a time, to ensure that we are all acting in ways that support these broader changes. This latter task is what the book is all about.

Before we can get into rethinking the practice of management we need to figure out what good management looks like in the first place. This is the subject of the next chapter.

— 2 —

SO WHAT IS GOOD MANAGEMENT REALLY?

Who was your best boss ever? And how about your worst boss? And why? If you have never answered this question, have a quick stab at it now. I have done this exercise with hundreds of people and the results are quite revealing – about you, as well as about the boss in question. Table 2.1 lists some typical answers.

We will come back to these examples – and your own experiences – later. The purpose of this chapter is to put some structure around the concept of good management. I will use plenty of specific examples, and I will also present some more systematic data that I collected over the last couple of years. If Chapter 1 was all about understanding the high-level argument that we need to improve the practice of management, this chapter makes the complementary case at the individual level. However, before getting into the meat of the story, I need to clarify a few pieces of terminology.

MANAGEMENT AND LEADERSHIP

I define management as *bringing people together to accomplish desired goals*. This definition works at two different levels. It applies to the

Table 2.1   What Makes a Good Boss? What Makes a Bad Boss?

Best boss

"Incredibly challenging and supportive at the same time. Pushed me beyond my comfort zone and held me accountable, but also cared about me as a person."

"He is incredibly supportive, goes out of his way to help me, has an infectious ability to create confidence in others."

"She made the team feel like a family – we are all in this together; she shielded us from top-down interference."

Worst boss

"He would go for people in a scheming, manipulative way, and wear them down."

"He was never available, just gave orders, his ideas were the only ones that counted; he cast a shadow over the team."

"She was autocratic, arrogant and imposing, not afraid to put people down in public; everyone was disposable."

collective activities of the people running an organization and it involves the development of formal and informal systems to enable effective coordination and decision-making. It also applies at an individual level – to the activities of each and every one of us as we go about our day-to-day work. In my previous book, *Reinventing Management*, I was concerned primarily with system-level management, and I argued that we might be able to develop better collective ways of working if we built our model of management from a different set of starting assumptions.

In this book I am focusing primarily on individual-level management – on the things you can do to bring a team of people together to accomplish your desired goals. Obviously this individual form of management does not happen in a vacuum, as the way you act is inevitably constrained by the formal and informal systems that surround you. But every manager has some degrees of freedom and chances are you have more space for discretionary behavior than you like to think you do. One of the themes of this book is about pushing back on, and even stretching, the invisible boundaries around your sphere of influence.

If management is about bringing people together to accomplish desired goals, leadership is a process of social influence. A leader is someone who is able to define and articulate a vision sufficiently clearly that others seek to follow them. Leadership is, to a large degree, about how a person presents him or herself to those around them and success is defined in terms of the quality and quantity of followers who he or she gains.

Management and leadership are therefore complementary activities, and to be effective in an executive role you need to be able to do both really well. It is often said that executives get into trouble because they are focused on management rather than leadership, meaning that they are too busy maintaining the status quo to develop a point of view on what needs to change. However, I think the reverse is equally true: some executives get into trouble because they are focused on leadership rather than management. In other words, they are so preoccupied with future opportunities, and with their image, that they lose touch with the day-to-day realities of the business they are running. The best executives, in my view, are those who are equally at home with both the big picture and the microlevel details. In the opinion of Jim Collins, they are adept at *zooming in and zooming out*. In the words of Standard Chartered CEO, Peter Sands, they are able to *swoop and soar*.

If you are a regular reader of business books, you will be familiar with the management versus leadership debate that has preoccupied academics for the best part of 30 years. In my view it is not just a tired debate, it also represents a false dichotomy. Indeed some languages, such as Swedish, have a single word (*ledarskap*) that covers both aspects of the executive's job. I have written extensively about this, but only because I feel the obsession with leadership has led to a dangerous diminution in the perceived importance in the practice of management.

All of which, hopefully, explains why this book is framed around management and not leadership. I am interested in how you can be more effective in your role, that is, bringing people together to accomplish desired goals. Some of what this involves may well be characterized as leadership, but that doesn't bother me in the slightest. What matters, of course, is that you figure out ways of being more effective in your work, not the label we put on those activities.

I also use the word "boss" quite frequently – not least in the book's title. Boss simply refers to the person or persons you report to (or how your team view you). While some people may feel that boss sounds too authoritarian or traditional, I don't mean it that way – I see it as a simple and neutral way of describing the person who sits above a subordinate in a hierarchical system.

BOSSES WE LOVE TO HATE

There are plenty of bad managers out there. I have had my share of small-minded, aloof, egotistical, thoughtless, short-fused (pick any combination) bosses, and my guess is most of you have as well. People usually find it much easier, and more fun, to talk about their "worst boss" than their "best boss," and that is why I typically start a discussion of management from this direction. I am not alone in this approach. Stanford Professor Bob Sutton has written two best-selling books – *The No Asshole Rule* and *Good Boss, Bad Boss* – with weird and wonderful accounts of how the workplace brings out the worst in some people. The reason that *Dilbert*, *The Office*, and *Fawlty Towers* are so funny is because they center on authority figures who are as oblivious to their own flaws as they are incompetent. A major Hollywood movie from 2011 was called *Horrible Bosses*. I have also contributed to the bad management debate using those old favorites, the Seven Deadly Sins (see Box 2.1).

Why this fascination with bad bosses? Partly, it is just about getting some light relief when work gets a bit tiresome. By swapping stories about the flaws of our managers, we are reassured that we are not alone, and we generate empathy from others. But bad bosses also provoke a sense of moral outrage in us, in the same way that we get upset about corrupt politicians or crooked policemen: bosses are authority figures, with responsibility for others, and as such they *should* behave better.

Bad bosses can also, potentially, be a useful source of insight. By playing up their worst flaws, we highlight the things we should not be doing ourselves. Indeed, it is often said that we learn more from failure

BOX 2.1   THE SEVEN DEADLY SINS OF MANAGEMENT

Here is my stab at defining what bad management looks like, using those old favorites, the Seven Deadly Sins. I developed these ideas during seminars with executives where we discussed their experiences of good and bad management. Of course, a bit of artistic licence is necessary here, to adapt words like "greed" and "lust" to corporate life, but on the whole I think they work pretty well. I have even put a little questionnaire together to help office workers across the land to rate their line manager. Does your boss succumb to only one or two of these sins? Or is he a seven-star sinner?

I have illustrated some of the sins with examples of famous Chief Executives, because these are stories we are all familiar with. But of course the sins apply at all management levels in the organization – they are as relevant to the first-line supervisor as they are to the big boss.

A **greedy** boss pursues wealth, status, and growth to get himself noticed. In short, he is an empire builder, and we don't have to look far to find examples of empire-building bosses. Perhaps the stand-out example today is Eike Batista, the Brazilian entrepreneur who has made the EBX Group (energy, mining, and logistics) into Brazil's fastest-growing company and him into the eighth-richest person in the world. Formerly married to a *Playboy* cover-girl and an ex-champion powerboat racer, he has now set his sights on becoming the first person in the world to amass a $100 billion fortune.

Lust is also about vanity projects – investments or acquisitions that make no rational sense, but play to the manager's desires. Edgar Bronfman, heir to the Seagram empire, leaps to mind here. To the "widespread astonishment" of the business world, he traded in the company's valuable holding in chemical giant Du Pont in order to buy up Universal Studios. A quick glimpse at his vitae helps explain his motives – even in his teens he was dabbling in song-writing and movie-making.

Wrath doesn't need a whole lot of explanation. "Chainsaw" Al Dunlap, Fred "the shred" Goodwin, and "Neutron" Jack Welch were all famous for losing their cool. We see this at all levels in the hierarchy – my first boss would turn bright red and start shaking before he yelled at some poor soul for failing to debug a piece of software properly.

Gluttony in the business world is where a manager puts too much on his proverbial plate. He needs to get involved in all decisions, he needs to be continuously updated, he never rests. We call this micromanaging and Gordon Brown did it during his brief stay at Number 10 Downing Street, where he insisted on reviewing minor departmental decisions and expenditures. It's not much fun working for such bosses, because they have a tendency, in Charles Handy's famous phrase, to "steal" your decisions. There is also a risk that

(Continued)

decision-making gets stuck: Lego CEO, Jurgen Knudstorp, notes that companies are far more likely to fail through "indigestion" than through "starvation," as Gordon Brown's Labour government discovered.

Healthy **pride** quickly tips over into hubris – an overestimation of your own abilities. In all the recent corporate crises – News International, Nokia, BP, even Toyota – there was tangible evidence of hubris in the manner and words of the executives at the top. Pride does, indeed, go before a fall. Perhaps the biggest tale of misplaced pride in recent years was Enron – its executives liked to think of themselves as the "smartest guys in the room" and they shortened the company's vision from becoming the "world's leading energy company" to becoming "the world's leading company." And we all know what happened there.

Envy manifests itself most clearly when a manager takes credit for the achievements of others. However, envy also rears its head in less obvious ways: when a manager chooses not to promote a rising star, for fear of showing up his own limitations, or when he keeps important information to himself, rather than sharing it with his team.

Sloth is workplace apathy – the managers who fall prey to sloth are simply not doing their job. They are inattentive, they don't communicate effectively, and they have no interest in their team's needs. Instead, they focus on their own comforts and, quite often, on personal interests outside of the workplace. We have all seen glimpses of sloth in the workplace: the boss who takes long lunch breaks but is "too busy" to sit down with us; the colleague who doesn't deliver on his part of a proposal; the executive who promises to get back to you on something but never does. Although sloth rarely makes it to the headlines, I suspect there are shades of sloth in most managers. The cost of sloth can be very high when management fails to make necessary strategic adjustments when the business is in crisis.

Rate Your Boss

If you are a boss (and most of us are), do your own self-assessment and figure out which of these sins you are most prone to. Remember – no-one is perfect and the chances are you are guilty of at least one of these sins. If you are brave, ask your own team to rate you, as a one-off exercise or as part of a broader 360-degree assessment process. The most challenging part is acting on the information you receive. However, the advantage of this approach, compared to other similar exercises, is that at least we can now put a label on what you are trying to avoid.

Answer the following seven questions for yourself or your current boss. Answer each question on a 1–5 scale, where 1 = "not at all" and 5 = "to a very large extent." Then count up the number of 4s and 5s – that tells you how many sins he or she is prone to.

1. To what extent do you/does your boss seek growth for growth's sake?

2. To what extent do you/does your boss pursue "pet" projects he/she is interested in, regardless of whether they fit with the organization's goals?

3. To what extent do you/does your boss become visibly angry at work when relatively small mistakes are made?

4. To what extent do you/does your boss get heavily involved in the details of all the projects he/she is responsible for?

5. To what extent do you/does your boss seek out recognition and plaudits for what he/she has achieved?

6. To what extent do you/does your boss try to take credit for the good work of others?

7. To what extent do you/does your boss organize things for his/her own convenience, rather than taking care of the needs and interests of others?

than from success, because it forces us to confront problems and change our behavior.

All of which is true. However, there are also a couple of reasons to be cautious with our focus on negative role models. First, *we have a tendency to accentuate the negative elements of a manager's personality when he has failed in a task,* just as we accentuate the positives when he has been successful. For example, up to his retirement in 2007, John Browne was lauded for transforming BP into a world-leading oil and gas company. Commentators praised his deep intellect, his decisive and bottom-line focused style, and his visionary leadership. Five years later, in the wake of the Macondo well disaster, the interpretation of John Browne's management style has been revised. He has been accused of "penny-pinching" and creating "dreadful bureaucracy and inefficiency," as well as being "aloof" and "a man highly unaware of the impact of his actions.[1]" Which one is the real John Browne? Well, there is some truth in both perspectives, but the point is that our interpretation is heavily skewed by how successful the person seems to be – the so-called "halo effect.[2]"

For another example of the same phenomenon, consider Box 2.2: Hero or Zero?, which features quotations about the leadership styles of Apple's former CEO Steve Jobs and Royal Bank of Scotland's former

BOX 2.2 HERO OR ZERO?

These quotes below are about two famous CEOs: Steve Jobs and Fred Goodwin. One is revered, the other is reviled. But their personalities and management styles were not a million miles apart. See if you can guess which of these quotes refer to Jobs and which to Goodwin[4].

1. "Most people were absolutely terrified of him. . . . He treated anyone who had a different view from his own with contempt."

2. "He applied charm or public humiliation in a way that in most cases proved to be pretty effective."

3. "He had a very impressive intellect . . . but he used that to bully those around him. People were intimidated from speaking their own mind because they feared his reaction."

4. "He would shout at a meeting, 'You asshole, you never do anything right.' It was like an hourly occurrence."

5. "Those meetings were never about enlightening anyone about anything. . . . It was all about humiliation."

6. "Very often, when told of a new idea, he will immediately attack it and say it is worthless, even stupid, and that it was a waste of time to work on it."

CEO Fred Goodwin. In many respects, the two leaders had similar styles – very pushy, forthright in their views, intolerant of failure, convinced of their own genius. However, because of the way history turned out, Jobs' style was deemed to be a key factor in his success, whereas Goodwin's style was interpreted as the seed of his downfall.

The underlying problem, then, is that many of the "bad" attributes of management are often beneficial to some degree. Intolerance of mediocrity helps to spur everyone on. Arguing can be a way of exposing the truth. Getting angry can be a way of making a point. Again, Steve Jobs is the classic example: as Debi Coleman, one of his team at Apple, recalls in his biography, "He would shout at a meeting, you asshole, you never do anything right, it was like an hourly occurrence. Yet I consider myself the absolute luckiest person in the world to have worked with him.[3]"

This leads to the second key point – that *what is defined as good or bad management depends on the personality and working style of the employee.* Debi Coleman loved working for Steve Jobs, because she could cope with his abrasive style and valued his ability to spur her to new heights. But many others couldn't handle him, or didn't want to put up with his childish outbursts. Jeff Raskin was one influential manager who parted ways with Jobs during the early years at Apple. In a parting shot to the board, Raskin wrote that Jobs "is a dreadful manager . . . he acts without thinking and with bad judgment . . . he does not give credit where due.[5]"

Of course, we have known for many years that one hallmark of a good boss is his or her ability to "personalize" their style to the needs and concerns of individual employees. Indeed, this ability to get inside the heads of your employees, to understand what makes them tick, is one of the key themes in this book. But the trouble is, these nuances often get lost in discussions about good and bad management, with the result that we fall back on what Jeff Pfeffer and Bob Sutton call *dangerous half-truths* – statements that are usually, but by no means always, true. So working for a "micromanaging" boss isn't usually much fun, but actually some people are reassured by having their work carefully reviewed, and in certain activities (brain surgery maybe, or nuclear waste disposal) micromanagement can be vitally important.

All of which serves to complicate our search for the secrets of good management. It can be valuable to learn from failure, by flagging up the qualities of management that we find loathsome or ineffectual. However, we have to do it carefully for two reasons: first, because many of the qualities of bad management are actually quite effective when used in moderation and, second, because what demotivates one person can actually be highly motivational for another.

WHAT MAKES A GOOD MANAGER? INSIGHTS FROM THE SURVEY

When I began working on this book two years ago, I was aware of all these challenges, and I was conscious that there appeared to be many different points of view on what constituted good or bad management. So I decided that it would be a good idea to gather some data of my own, to help me figure out the truth. To stay consistent with the emerging theme of the book, I thought the best people to ask would be employees. Working with colleagues[6], I conducted interviews with more than 50 people, asking them about what made their bosses effective or ineffective. Armed with hundreds of pages of interview notes, I then developed a survey, which included a long set of questions about the good and bad things managers do. This was filled in by almost 1000 people across more than 10 companies.

Here are the key findings from the survey. First, I asked the respondents to indicate how much their boss exhibited what we might call the eight good habits of effective managers (see Figure 2.1). Here are the average scores for these eight habits. Top of the list was "always available to talk" and "good at providing support when I need it"; bottom of the list (but still with an average score of more than 3 out of 5) were "structures for projects to make them interesting and challenging" and "looking for ways to help me improve my effectiveness."

Next, I turned things around, and asked respondents about the seven *bad habits* that had emerged from the interviews (Figure 2.2). In other words, I wanted to know how much their bosses were engaging in ineffectual management practices – on the basis that we can learn as much from failure as from success. Interestingly, one bad

Figure 2.1   Positive Attributes of My Line Manager

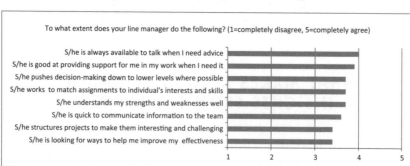

Figure 2.2 Negative Attributes of My Line Manager

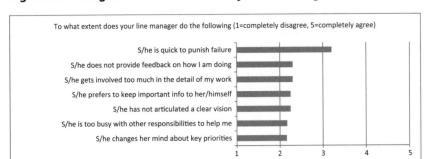

habit stuck out above all the rest with a rating, above the mid-point of three: the boss is "too quick to punish failure." All the other bad habits rated much lower, between 2.2 and 2.4 on a five-point scale. Notice, also, that by looking at the good habits and bad habits together, we see both sets of behaviors coexisting. For example, the respondents said their bosses were always available and good at providing support, but they also saw quite a lot of evidence that the same bosses were "too busy with other responsibilities to help me" and "do not provide me with feedback on how I am doing." As I said earlier, management is a messy subject.

These charts tell us what the respondents saw their managers doing. Of course, it doesn't tell us much at all about whether these habits were actually effective. I might see my boss making him or herself readily available to give me advice, but if I am happy to work on my own, then I won't value this effort. So to sharpen up the analysis, I asked the respondent a key question: *How likely is it that you would recommend your line manager to a colleague, as someone they should work for in the future* (1 = not at all, 10 = extremely likely)? I then used statistical analysis to identify which of the good and bad habits listed above were the most important in explaining whether a respondent would recommend his or her manager to others. Table 2.2 lists the results. The ones on the left are the top three things you look for in a manager: when your manager is doing these things, you recommend him or her to your friends as someone they should work for. The ones on the right, on the other hand, are the top three bad habits: when

Table 2.2   The Most Important Positive and Negative Attributes of a Manager

Ranked list of "good habits" that predict whether respondents would *encourage* their friends to work for this manager	Ranked list of "bad habits" that predict whether respondents would *discourage* their friends from working for this manager
1. S/he is good at providing support for me in my work when I need it	1. S/he prefers to keep important information to her/himself
2. S/he pushes decision-making down to lower levels wherever possible	2. S/he has not articulated a clear vision
3. S/he understands my strengths and weaknesses well	3. S/he is quick to punish failure

your manager is doing these things, you encourage your friends to find someone else to work for.

This analysis helped me to close in on what the people filling out the questionnaire thought was really important. The best managers, in their view, are the ones who give their employees space to make decisions, who provide them with support, and who understand what they are capable of. The worst managers, on the other hand, are secretive with information, they don't articulate a clear sense of direction, and they punish failure.

ANOTHER PERSPECTIVE: INSIGHTS FROM SEMINAR DISCUSSIONS

These data provided me with a provisional set of conclusions. However, I wanted to try a different approach as well, to see if the same story emerged. So over about 18 months, I incorporated an exercise into my management seminars that I picked up from Henry Stewart, CEO of Happy Ltd. First, I said to them, *think back to the last time you were fully engaged and motivated at work; what were the key features of that piece of work?* Regardless of whether I was working with a board of directors, front-line employees, high-school teachers, or research scientists, the same points emerged. People were engaged when their work was challenging, when it addressed an important issue, when they had freedom to figure things out for themselves, when they were working with high-quality colleagues, and when they felt their contribution was recognized.

Then I asked them a supplementary question. *In the light of this discussion, put on your manager "hat": what should you do to ensure your employees are fully engaged and motivated?* A couple of insights quickly emerged. First, the majority of employees don't want a whole lot of "managing" – they want space, challenge, and opportunity. So the boss has to be thoughtful about when he intervenes and in the type of interventions that he makes. Second, a large part of the manager's job is about structuring the work in advance, so that its importance to the organization is clear, it is sufficiently challenging to get the employee interested, and it allows the employee to work with other good people. Managers also have a coaching and supporting role to play here, providing feedback and resources as needed during the project, and recognition for a job well done afterwards.

There were two frequent grumbles when I did this exercise. Some people felt this approach didn't apply to them. "This is all well and good if you work in new product development," said one mid-level manufacturing manager, "but my people are sitting on a production line and their work is intrinsically boring. So this model doesn't help me." My response was, yes, it is much easier to provide your employees with freedom and challenge in some jobs than others, but that doesn't prevent you from looking for creative ways of making production-line work less boring than usual.

The other grumble was that this model was too, well, nice. "Is the best teacher the one who lets his students figure out what they are going to do?" asked one senior airline executive, in a slightly oblique manner. His point, of course, was that good teachers don't just give their students space to figure things out; they also provide very clear targets, they provide instruction, they evaluate their students, and they aren't afraid to hand out failing grades, and to punish them if they fail to show up for class. I am not personally convinced the analogy to high school is a good one (employees and students are motivated by very different things) but, setting that aside, the airline executive was making a good point. The exercise was built on an assumption that employees want to do a good job and they simply need a "context" in which to do it. While this is likely the case for the vast majority of employees, managers still have to have the skills and tools to deal with recalcitrant or ill-equipped employees.

In terms of developing my own point of view on what good management looks like, these were important points. Not all work is intrinsically interesting, so there are limits to how far you can push a model built on employee engagement. And good managers aren't just softies who let their people do what they want – sometimes they have to take tough decisions and make unpopular judgments. Both these points will resurface at various times throughout the book.

The interesting thing, however, in doing this exercise in dozens of management seminars, is how similar the story was to what came out of the large-sample survey. By pulling the insights from the two methodologies together, I ended up with the following five hallmarks of a good manager:

1. *Gives employees challenging work to do.* The manager believes in the employee's desire to do a good job and his capacity to improve, and deliberately gives him work to do that stretches him. A couple of the people I interviewed during this research captured this nicely: "She gave me incredibly challenging work and made me believe I could do it" and "He gave us real responsibility . . . he allowed people to make mistakes."

2. *Creates space for them to do it.* A large part of the manager's job is simply to let go – to give the employee the space to figure things out for herself and to learn through those experiences. "He gave us real responsibility . . . he allowed people to make mistakes," was one comment I heard.

3. *Provides support when needed.* The manager doesn't interfere, but makes herself available, offering feedback and access to resources when needed. Typical quotes from the interviews were as follows: "he provided learning pathways for everyone," "she worked with me to find a solution," "he shielded me from

others," and "he knows how to give feedback well, both good and bad."

4. *Gives recognition and praise.* The manager makes a point of giving positive feedback when a piece of work is done well, and makes sure others realize what the employee has achieved. Typical quotes from the research were: "She always gave me credit for my achievements"; and "at times he offered us small, unexpected gifts as signs of appreciation."

5. *Is not afraid to make tough decisions.* Sometimes difficult things have to be done, such as downsizing a team, dealing with harassment or bullying, or firing a poor performer, and often these are the times when the manager shows real strengths. "She makes difficult decisions palatable" was one comment I heard. The manager also knows employees well enough to know how hard to push them. For example: "He is strong on performance management: he lets you know when things are going well and when they are not."

I showed this list to people who had been involved in the research and they confirmed it was a nice summary of what they had intuitively figured out for themselves. But it gradually dawned on me that there was nothing remotely novel or surprising about it. I observed my colleagues at London Business School teaching and I saw them making all the same points. I re-read some recent best-selling business books, such as Dan Pink's *Drive* and Bob Sutton's *Good Boss, Bad Boss*, and I went back to some of the classics, such as Peter Drucker's *Management* and Mary Parker Follet's *The New State*, and again all the same qualities of good management were there. Then I read about Google's Project Oxygen, as described in the introduction, and how their extensive, data-driven approach had yielded essentially the same set of findings, yet again.

So my search for "what makes a good manager" was over. I had the answer, but so did everyone else. There was no mystery to be solved, no hidden qualities that needed to be uncovered. Perhaps there was no book to be written here after all.

THE RHETORIC AND THE REALITY

Rather than give up, I decided to take a different approach. As the old adage has it, "If everyone is thinking the same, that means someone is not thinking." So if a generation of researchers has all come up with the same advice, but that advice is not being followed, that opens up an opportunity to understand why. So the interesting question is not: *What is good management?* Rather, the question is: *Given that we know what good management is, why on earth don't we do it?*

Of course this is not a completely novel question either. In a general sense, there have been lots of studies attempting to close this "knowing doing" gap between what individuals and organizations recognize they should do and what they actually do. It is also called a rhetoric-reality gap or an analysis–execution gap. Moving beyond the field of business, there are entire subdisciplines of psychology and sociology that are focused on helping people to do what they know they should, be it weight loss, giving up smoking, or being a better parent.

Strangely enough, the field management research hasn't really got a good answer to this question yet. For example, a fascinating study undertaken by the Krauthammer Institute revealed enormous gaps between what employees wanted from their managers versus what they actually got[7]. For example, 89% of respondents wanted their managers to give them autonomy when delegating, but only 28% got this; 74% of respondents wanted their manager to let them finish explaining their idea before interrupting, but only 23% said this is what happened. The gaps here are staggering and, as the study says, "managers continue to display real difficulties on a range of fundamental skills."

Insights from my own research have also highlighted the size of the gap. Employees want challenging and interesting work to do, but they often get confusing and unclear objectives. They want space to learn and experiment, but they often get a micromanaging and meddling boss who is constantly peering over their shoulder. Table 2.3 lists the five hallmarks of a good manager from earlier, and contrasts it with the more typical behaviors that are exhibited in the workplace.

Table 2.3   What Employees Want and What They Get

What employees want	What employees often get
1. **Challenging work to do**	*Confusing or unclear objectives* "He is unreasonable, he would like everything immediately." "Goals were blurry, at best; she couldn't prioritize."
2. **Space to work**	*Micromanagement and meddling* "He paid obsessive attention to every single detail. He could not assign the right priorities to tasks. He didn't give a modicum of trust."
3. **Support when needed**	*A selfish boss, focused on his own agenda* "He did not tell us the decisions made during meetings." "He imposed his own thinking without any explanation." "He never gave time, said he was too busy, concerned only with his own well-being." "He was emotionally detached – I came to work in a leg plaster and he didn't even ask what happened to me."
4. **Recognition and praise**	*Limited and mostly negative feedback* "He would wear us down with poisonous remarks and would pick on certain people." "Lots of shouting and a lack of respect for those around him."
5. **A manager who is not afraid to make tough decisions**	*A manager who dithers* "She couldn't make a decision and always seemed to follow the advice of the last person she spoke to."

I often show this chart in seminars and ask the participants why there is so much bad management out there, given that we know what we should be doing. The first few answers are very predictable.

Some people say they don't have time – they are so busy doing other, more important, things that the time and effort required to be an effective manager gets squeezed out. Others say they are being pulled in too many different directions – they would love to carefully structure a project for one of their team, but their own manager keeps changing his mind about what is needed. A third common response is to say how difficult it is to get the right balance – one employee wants very little help, the next wants a lot more, so you have to tailor your approach to the particular needs of each person who works for you.

All of which is true – up to a point. But I simply don't buy the argument that we are "too busy" to implement many of these good management practices. Some of them (recognition and praise, for example) take virtually no time; others (structuring work clearly, for example) take a bit of time but typically save more time later. And of course a great deal of the work many managers spend their time on could – and probably should – be delegated to their employees. In fact, delegation often serves a double purpose – it gives your employees new and often interesting tasks to do and it frees up your time as well.

So I think we need to look beyond these superficial reasons why we don't do what we know we should. We need to dig deeper and to challenge some of our underlying assumptions about what our employees want, and how we and they look at the world. This "employee's eye view" is the subject of the next chapter.

— 3 —

GETTING INSIDE THE MINDS OF YOUR EMPLOYEES: WHAT MAKES THEM TICK?

Do you think you understand your employees? Do you pride yourself on your empathy and your insight into what makes them tick? Most of us would like to answer yes to these questions, but the evidence says that we would be wrong to do so.

Consider the example of Mike, a senior HR manager at an auto parts factory in the north of England. He had been drafted in from the US parent company, Motor Co, to help implement a new set of manufacturing practices, but after a year he was pulling his hair out: "Coming here has been a nightmare and a complete career disaster," was his exasperated comment, "this is one of the most militant shops I've ever seen, but none of it's union activity."

Mike's experiences are recounted in a fascinating study by three UK academics, Mahmoud Ezzamel, Hugh Wilmott, and Frank Worthington, called "Power, control and resistance in 'the factory that time forgot'.[1]" It is a story of an old-fashioned British firm, Northern Plant, with manufacturing practices "at least ten years behind the times." Its workers were clever, but suspicious of change. They understood what was possible far better than the plant's managers, and as a result the managers would tolerate what games the workers played, as long as production levels were maintained.

Into this mix came Mike and his American colleagues, following the acquisition by Motor Co. All sorts of modern work practices, from Toyota-style lean production through to cellular manufacturing, were brought over. For Mike, these were proven practices that would benefit the plant workers as well as providing efficiency gains. However, for the old hands at Northern Plant, they were an unwelcome intrusion into their established order.

The workers were too savvy to actively resist the new practices. Instead, they responded with what the researchers called "sustained yet overtly accommodating resistance." They delayed the creation of work teams by arguing about how they should be put together, they challenged the new performance metrics for not being valid, and they spread disharmony among the managers by showing how they had been stabbing each other in the back. Worst of all, these various tactics for resisting change were not consistent across the factory. Mike, the American HR professional, was used to formal union activity and he had experience in dealing with it, but he had no idea how to cope with this form of "disorganized resistance.[2]"

GETTING INSIDE THE MIND OF THE EMPLOYEE

So what is the point of this slightly quaint tale of scheming, intransigent workers and impotent managers? Obviously Northern Plant is not a typical factory and it is rare for managers to find themselves in Mike's shoes, dropped into an alien world with few familiar reference points.

However, most of us have had occasional Mike-like experiences, where we have struggled to understand our employees' behavior. I recall an instance when I had just taken on my first proper managerial job. I was full of bright ideas for changes we could make. I sent an email out to my team, suggesting a complete rethinking of the structure of the team and how I wanted their input in the redesign. The response was complete silence: no-one replied to the email and no-one mentioned it in the next daily catch-up meeting either. I knew I had done something wrong, but I had no idea what. Eventually, after some prompting from me, the most senior person in the team gave me some advice: "Your ideas are too radical for this team; some of them are very risk-averse. They need to get to know you properly before you start a conversation like this." Suitably chastened, I resolved to be a bit more thoughtful before proposing my next bright idea – and to get to know my team better.

This chapter is a "deep dive" into the mind of the employee, to shed some light on what makes him or her tick? Two cautionary notes before we get started. First, it is difficult to write about the employee without sounding a little bit patronizing. This is not my intention. Rather, I will attempt to stand back a little and to adopt an analytical approach. The subsequent chapters (Chapters 4 through 6) will provide plenty of practical advice, but this chapter will be a bit more academic in its tone.

Second, my bias in this chapter will be towards understanding employees in poorly paid, tedious jobs, where the contrast between the attitude of the boss and employee is typically the greatest. Some managers have never experienced such jobs; others started their careers in this sort of work but have forgotten what it felt like. Either way, these are the jobs where the worldview of the employee is hardest for a seasoned manager to relate to. Of course, the sceptical reader will also note that I, as an academic, may also find it hard to get my head inside the worldview of an employee in a poorly paid, tedious job. Fair enough. So to prepare for this chapter, I spent a lot of time interviewing and working with front-line employees, in a hotel chain, a call center, a mining company, and a building company. I also developed a questionnaire to get their perspectives, filled out by almost 1000 people.

The chapter looks at four aspects of the employee's worldview: motivations, fears, strengths, and identity (Figure 3.1).

Figure 3.1   Four Aspects of the Employee's Worldview

IDENTITY

Let's start with identity, because it is the most central, as well as the most puzzling, part of the story. If we go back to the workers at Northern Plant, their behavior didn't make much sense from Mike's corporate viewpoint. After all, the new practices he was trying to implement were going to make the plant more productive (thereby safeguarding jobs) *and* they were supposed to help workers develop broader skillsets and become more involved in their work. Unfortunately, the workers didn't see it that way – what they saw was a threat to the identity they had developed for themselves over many years. A central part of this identity was *autonomy*, that is, the freedom to sort out their own problems as long as they hit their production targets. New management practices of Motor Co threatened this autonomy – it required workers to buy in to new practices and new measures that they would not have control over. So the most natural way of retaining their self-identity was to push back – to use whatever tricks and techniques they could muster to keep the new practices at bay. The importance of retaining a clear sense of identity was, somewhat surprisingly, more important than concerns for the long-term viability of the plant.

So the first big insight for you as a manager is that you need to get to grips with your employees self-identity: how they see their role in the workplace. The trouble is, identity is a slippery thing. An employee's identity evolves over time, as a function of his or her experiences, responsibilities, and relationships. Most people don't actually take the time to articulate – even to themselves – what their identity is. There are some simple stereotypes that we can quickly recognize: the ambitious MBA graduate who will do whatever it takes to climb the corporate ladder; the high-school teacher who loves helping kids learn; or the immigrant who works two minimum-wage jobs to pay for his or her kid's education. These individuals have no trouble making sense of their role in the workplace. But for the vast majority of employees, identity is much more fuzzy and open to interpretation.

Understanding the self-identity of your employees therefore requires a certain amount of detective work. There is no simple categorization scheme you can use, so you have to divine how workers see themselves by observing their reaction to changes in their working environment. Here is another example drawn from an academic research study[3], a story about the introduction of self-managed teams in Stitchco, a UK clothing manufacturer, in the 1990s. As with Northern Plant, the logic of shifting from an old-fashioned piecework system to a new team-based production system seemed entirely obvious to top management, as it would help the factory to increase its output, while also providing workers with a broader range of skills. By providing a base rate of pay and team-based incentives, they believed the new system would also make the workers financially better off.

However, the mostly-female workforce hated the change. The more experienced workers found themselves carrying the newer ones and working harder than before in order to reach their team bonus targets. Some of them were asked to become supervisors, but they found it hard to start telling their co-workers what to do. Many of them liked to be able to set their own pace, perhaps working harder one day and more slowly the next day, and the team-based system made this much harder to do.

Again, a well-intentioned change hit resistance because management failed to understand the self-identity of the workforce. In this case, the female employees at Stitchco were operating in very narrowly defined jobs with no autonomy over what they did. But they did have control over one important part of their work, namely the speed with which they worked. They also enjoyed the banter of the shopfloor, being mates with their fellow machinists. The teamwork model threatened both these features – some women found themselves overseeing their mates, which created tension, while others resented having to worry about the bonuses of their mates in deciding how fast to work.

Management at Stitchco gradually got their heads around these problems, and while they didn't get rid of the teamwork system altogether they scaled back some elements, for example, by providing supervisors rather than forcing the women on the shopfloor to assume these roles. Performance in the factory gradually improved, though not as quickly as top management would have liked.

So what's the bottom line here? Simply that all employees have a way of making sense of the things they do and why they do them, and that it is much easier to get things done when you reinforce, rather than challenge, this sense of identity. Good managers are detectives – they look for clues about which initiatives their employees get excited about and which ones they resist, and they gradually build up a picture of their employees' identity.

MOTIVATIONS

Motivation is the condition in an employee that activates his or her behavior and gives it direction; it is what drives the employee to spend time and energy on a particular task or goal. Unlike identity, which is poorly understood and rarely discussed, motivation is a topic of which every manager has at least a basic understanding[4].

Employees are motivated by an enormous range of things. In an earlier book, I distinguished between three drivers of discretionary effort from employees:

- Material drivers, including salary, bonuses, promotions, and prizes

- Social drivers, including recognition for achievement, status, and having good colleagues

- Personal drivers, including freedom to act, the opportunity to build expertise, and working for a worthwhile cause

While all of these drivers matter, they are not equally important. It has been shown, for example, that materials drivers (also called extrinsic rewards) have very little influence over a certain threshold level, whereas social and personal drivers (intrinsic rewards) can be extremely powerful at all levels. Material drivers are also known to crowd out other drivers – give an investment banker the promise of a large bonus and all other things get ignored.

As part of my research for this book, I polled almost 1000 employees to ask about the importance of various sources of motivation. Figure 3.2 shows the overall scores. True to expectation, employees say that the most important things for them in a job are intellectual challenge, opportunities for advancement, and working for good

Figure 3.2 What Motivates Employees?

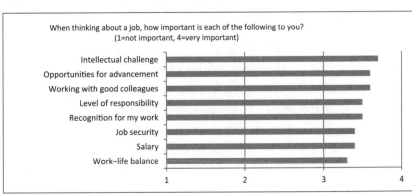

colleagues. Salary, as usual, is seen as relatively unimportant compared to these personal and social drivers.

These findings echo the story from the last chapter. Good managers, you will recall, provide their employees with challenging work, space to act, support when needed, and recognition. Not surprisingly, these are the very same features that employees seek in their work. Many other studies have come up with similar findings.

However, this isn't the whole story. I have always had a nagging concern that this emphasis on intellectual challenge and personal advancement is a little, well, idealistic. We know from Maslow's famous Hierarchy of Needs that such higher-order needs are only valid once someone has covered all their more basic needs. And what if these findings were nothing more than a reflection of our own values and biases as researchers? After presenting these ideas a couple of years ago, an executive we will call John came up to me: "This is good stuff, Julian, but you are looking at the wrong people. You should be studying people with shit jobs. That is where the real challenge lies."

John had hit upon an important point. When you look at the full spectrum of jobs in the economy, the ones with intrinsically high levels of satisfaction are few in number (see Box 3.1: Job Satisfaction versus Pay). It is relatively easy, as a manager, to end up with happy and engaged employees when they are doing work they might choose as a hobby. It is also relatively easy to devise motivation schemes when there are opportunities for large salary increments and bonuses. The challenging jobs, from a managers' perspective, are the ones with low pay and low intrinsic satisfaction – things like burger flipping, hotel room cleaning, or working on a production line or in a call center.

So what are the motivators for people working in these types of jobs? Here is one simple piece of analysis. From my survey, I extracted the average scores for three companies. Drill Co is a mining company, and the respondents were front-line employees in a basic processing operation. Call Co is an IT services company and the respondents were call center workers. In other words, both groups were in John's category of "shit jobs." For the sake of contrast, Bank Co is a financial services company and the respondents were recent MBA graduates in white-collar jobs with good promotion prospects.

Figure 3.3 Motivation Levels in Three Different Companies

	DRILLCO	BANKCO	CALLCO
NEED FOR MONEY			
• Salary	3.5	3.5	3.2
NEED FOR PERSONAL ACHIEVEMENT			
• Intellectual challenge	2.8	3.8	3.7
• Opportunities for advancement	3.0	3.8	3.3
• Level of responsibility	3.1	3.8	3.7
• Recognition for my work	3.8	4.3	4.3
NEED FOR SOCIAL AFFILIATION			
• Working with good colleagues	3.6	3.8	3.7
• Job security	3.8	2.8	2.8
• Work–life balance	3.9	3.1	3.1

The differences in scores across the three companies are significant (see Figure 3.3). In my interpretation, Drill Co's employees are stuck in a job with few prospects for growth or promotion, so they don't waste their energy worrying about those things. They value recognition for a job well done, but their highest motivators are for the various aspects of social affiliation – working with good colleagues, job security, and work–life balance. Their identity, rather like the people at Northern Plant, is wrapped up in their colleagues and the community in which they are working. Bank Co's employees, on the other extreme, are ambitious and eager to please. They have a very high need for personal achievement – because they know it can be accommodated in this company – and they have much less concern for job security and work–life balance at this point in their working lives. Call Co's employees, despite being in poorly paid and tedious jobs, are actually more like Bank Co's employees in terms of what motivates them. This might appear surprising, but one important reason is that the company is growing quickly, so there are many promotion opportunities.

BOX 3.1   JOB SATISFACTION VERSUS PAY

Not all jobs were created equally when it comes to motivation. I dug into the statistics on employment across the UK and this allowed me to put together a chart comparing the average salary and job satisfaction level for every job category in the country (Figure 3.4)[6]. If we simply divide this chart into four boxes, we get the following results. Box 1 is the people whose hobby is also their job – the hairdressers, vicars, and fitness trainers. They aren't well paid, but they love what they do so they aren't so bothered about money. Box 2 is the well-paid and highly satisfied group, often professionals such as architects, scientists, or senior executives. Box 3 is the well-paid but unsatisfied group, which includes many subsectors of the IT industry, commissioned salespeople, and the lower levels of professional hierarchies such as law, accountancy, and banking. As an academic working in a business school, I have plenty of friends in each of these boxes, and I can easily make sense of their motivations, aspirations, and concerns.

Figure 3.4   UK Jobs Rated by Job Satisfaction and Average Salary

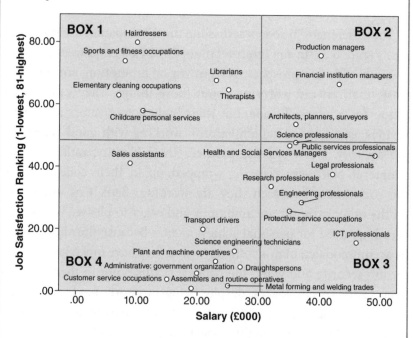

Box 4 is perhaps the most important one. Working in a factory or call center or hotel or McDonalds is poorly paid work, and not a whole lot of fun, and of course there are far more people, in absolute numbers, working in Box 4 than any of the other boxes. If we are concerned about the societal benefits of improving the quality of management, as discussed in Chapter 1, then this is the biggest opportunity area. It is also the biggest challenge: when employees are intrinsically motivated (Box 1) or their extrinsic rewards are high (Box 3), the "levers" the manager can pull to get more out of them are pretty well understood, but motivating employees when their work is neither intrinsically or extrinsically satisfying is far from straightforward.

These data provide us with a slightly more nuanced view of employee motivation. Yes, it is true that employees are motivated by work that gives them a sense of purpose, freedom to make mistakes, and opportunities to develop, but there are a great many jobs where these features are simply not available. In such cases, employees are pragmatic and flexible. They don't yearn for things that aren't on offer; instead, they focus on those aspects of their working lives that they have some control over, and they seek to make improvements there[5].

For example, I found myself working on the front desk in a hotel chain in London, in the Summer of 2011, alongside two thirty-something Romanian immigrants. They were articulate, thoughtful women, one with a degree in Accounting, both with children, and they were broadly happy with their work, despite the minimum-wage pay scale. I asked them about why they did this work and what motivated them. They didn't linger on the need for intellectual challenge in their work or the importance of responsibility over others. Instead, their answers focused on the opportunities to do overtime, the training courses on offer, the quality of their colleagues, and the opportunity to bring their children up in London. These were all motivators, in other words, that were within reach. These women had scaled back their ambitions in certain areas and shifted their ambitions to match the identity that they had taken on in the workplace.

In sum, employees are motivated by a complex set of factors. As a manager, it is important to understand the near-universal desire for challenging, autonomous work that allows an individual to develop their skills. But it is also important to look more closely at the specific circumstances the employees find themselves in, because those circumstances will lead some motivators to be enhanced and others suppressed.

FEARS

Compared to motivation, fear gets much less attention in studies of the workplace. And yet it is perhaps an equally important driver of behavior. One employee I interviewed for this book described his organization as follows: "We live in a culture of fear, we keep our heads down, trying to avoid doing anything to upset [the boss]. Sometimes everything is fine, but then he will blow up at someone because they made a copying mistake, and the whole office is affected." I talked in the previous chapter about the "seven deadly sins" of management and how poisonous an angry or greedy boss can be for the rest of the organization. But even in a relatively well-managed workplace, there is still a lot of fear under the surface – fear of looking foolish when you make a presentation, fear of not performing up to expectations, fear of losing your job if the company gets into trouble.

Quality guru Edwards Deming was one writer who picked up on the importance of fear. In his famous list of 14 principles, number 8 was the need to *Drive out Fear* in the workplace[7]. "No-one can put in his best performance unless he feels secure," Deming wrote, "and secure means without fear, not afraid to express ideas, not afraid to ask questions."

So what are manifestations of fear in the workplace? In doing the research for this book, I drew up a list of 14 potential sources of fear and put them into my survey. The chart in Figure 3.5 lists them in order.

I discussed these fears with many of my interview subjects. What became apparent, very quickly, was the enormous diversity of answers to my question "What is your biggest fear or concern?" One person said her biggest concern was not being able to pay her team the size of bonuses they were expecting (yes, she was a banker); another was worried about the stress he was under because of the long hours

Figure 3.5   Sources of Fear in the Workplace

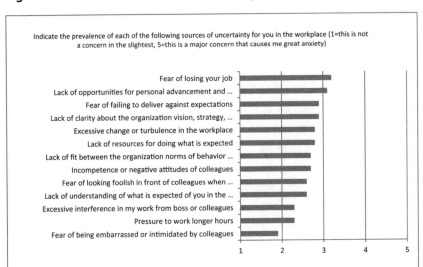

required in his job; a third was worried about a rumoured downsizing and the possibility that he might lose his job.

I quickly realized that what counts as fear depends on the situation the employee is in. Some people were focused on very basic fears, such as losing their job, others had what we might call higher-order concerns, such as not living up to their own expectations, or not getting the level of mentoring they would like.

This insight then led to the concept of a "Hierarchy of Fears" in organizations that mirrors Abraham Maslow's famous "Hierarchy of Needs." Thus, the basic fear of losing one's job is analogous to the need for food and shelter; then once this fear has been alleviated, other fears or concerns, such as not fitting in as well as one might like or not getting the personal development opportunities one craves, start to surface. The four levels can be described as follows:

- *Level 1: need for security and safety in the workplace.* This need manifests itself primarily in a *fear of redundancy*: "My major concern is about the future of this company: once this project finishes, I am not sure what I would end up doing." A related fear is *concern with excessive turbulence and change*: "My biggest fears are that our company is understaffed, that as we move ahead we find ourselves unprepared to deal with such a huge amount of work."

- *Level 2: need for affiliation to a group.* This need is linked to two fears. One is a *concern about not fitting in.* "I find the forced agreeableness of the culture disturbing, I am not good at this," said one person. "The things I work on and see as strategic priorities do not match what the company sees as a priority," said another. The other is what we might call a *frustration with ineffective processes*, in that they compromise the quality of the working environment. "What demotivates me is poor organization of work . . . sometimes the company is excessively bureaucratic, which slows the work-flow down significantly," was one person's biggest concern. Another said, "I am worried that we spend a lot of time firefighting and doing dismal time-wasting projects."

- *Level 3: need for personal achievement.* This need links to several fears. One is a *fear of failing to deliver on high expectation*: "One of my biggest anxieties is about assignments not completely finished." The second is a *fear of looking incompetent.* "I worry about looking stupid in front of others, of not performing," was one person's biggest fear. The third is a *concern with the stress of work*, in that stress is typically a by-product of working hard and setting high expectations. One person described it thus: "The worst aspect of my job is the stress that derives from the unpredictability of the workload. . . . I think such tensions cascade down from the top."

- *Level 4: need for self-actualization.* This need links to a concern about the *lack of opportunities for personal development.* "My current role is too limited in scope, it doesn't utilize my broader skillset . . . my line manager is in another location, which affects my career progression" and "I am worried my

Figure 3.6   Fears and Uncertainties in Three Companies

	DRILLCO	BANKCO	CALLCO
SELF-ACTUALIZATION			
• Lack of opportunities for personal advancement and development	3.4	3.2	2.5
PERSONAL ACHIEVEMENT			
• Fear of failing to deliver against expectations	3.6	3.4	2.8
• Fear of looking foolish in front of your colleagues when something doesn't go well	3.0	2.8	2.0
AFFILIATION TO GROUP			
• Lack of fit between the organization's values/norms of behavior and my own	3.6	2.5	2.7
• Lack of clarity about the organization's vision, strategy and performance	3.9	2.5	2.1
SAFETY AND SECURITY			
• Excessive change and turbulence in the workplace	4.1	2.6	2.5
• Fear of losing your job	4.2	2.3	1.6

boss [who is an excellent mentor] may leave" were two typical comments here.

So how can you make use of this hierarchy of fears? Again, it is useful to compare the answers given in three of the companies in my research to see how they vary (see Figure 3.6). At Drill Co (the mining company), there is a high level of angst among the employees. Their scores are higher than average across the board but, more importantly, their fears are highest at "Level 1" in the hierarchy. Put simply, they are worried about their jobs, because the company is in a very precarious position, and this means that all the higher-order concerns about affiliation, personal achievement, and self-actualization are just not that important. As a manager at Drill Co, you would want to resolve these basic fears as soon as possible, and you wouldn't want to invest a great deal of effort on the higher-order concerns until you had done so.

Bank Co (the financial services company) is in a very different position. The biggest concerns its employees have are failing to deliver against expectations and lack of opportunities for personal development and growth. The ratings for fears at the lower level of the hierarchy are significantly lower. It is easy to make sense of this story, as Bank Co is full of ambitious, young employees who feel secure in their work (and their ability to get another job if this one doesn't pan out), so are worried only about the higher-order parts of the hierarchy. As a manager at Bank Co, your time is likely to be spent coaching and supporting these individuals to help them achieve their potential, and assuring the best ones that this company will help them develop further.

Call Co (the call center operator) has a more balanced profile than the other two and seems to be a relatively worry-free place, with ratings lower than average across the board. The biggest concerns are a fear of failing to deliver and a concern about lack of fit with the company's norms, but taken as a whole there are very few "red flags" here. As a manager at Call Co, you would want to invest some time on cultural issues, making sure employees understood what was expected of them, and on coaching and supporting the people who are looking for bigger responsibilities.

By profiling your employees' fears and concerns in this way, you can draw some useful inferences about how to prioritize your efforts as a manager. Of course it's worth remembering that every individual has a slightly different set of concerns – these are aggregate figures that obscure as much as they reveal.

It is also worth keeping in mind that the hierarchy of fears applies only to the workplace, and work is only one part of an individual's life. Some people seek to satisfy most of their needs through work; others rely on their family and their nonwork activities to address the various elements of Maslow's pyramid. For example, many people choose to start their own business to achieve esteem and self-actualization, but of course without any job security. In such cases, they derive their security from other sources, typically a supportive family. So the workplace cannot satisfy all an employee's needs, but we believe it has the potential to satisfy many of them. It is up to us, as managers, to decide how many of the elements of the hierarchy of needs we want to satisfy for our employees.

STRENGTHS

The final part of the framework for making sense of the employee's worldview is strengths – or more broadly the things an individual does well, or less well, in the workplace. It has become fashionable to talk about strengths largely thanks to Marcus Buckingham's influential research[8]. He has observed that as employees and as managers we spend a lot of time – too much time – identifying and working on our weaknesses. It is human nature, he observes, to pick out the worst grade in a report card and to try to improve it, but it is the wrong response. First, we will never take our weaknesses and turn them into strengths; second, life is too short to spend all our time working on things we are not very good at. Instead, we should figure out what our strengths are and we should play to them – we should build them up further and we should find work opportunities that allow us to use them to the fullest. For companies, the challenge is to build a better fit between employees' strengths and the jobs they do. For example, rather than define jobs first and fill them with suitable people, we should start with our people and design jobs around their proven strengths.

Many companies have worked with Marcus Buckingham's "strength-finder" methodology and some have developed them further. For example, HCL Technologies, the Indian IT services company, has a tool called EPIC – Employee Passion Indicative Count – which it uses to track the aspects of an employee's work that he is passionate about (I will describe this in more detail in Chapter 4). This analysis helps managers to place their team members into the appropriate jobs, and even to help employees shape their own roles.

During the research for this book I was drawn to the idea that we should take employee's strengths more seriously, so in my survey I asked the respondents about how good they were at various aspects of their work. Their responses are given in Figure 3.7.

I must admit, I found these ratings rather puzzling when I first saw them. It is no surprise really that people rated themselves as above average on everything – it is well known that people tend to have an overly rosy picture of their own capabilities, whether it is driving a car

Figure 3.7   Employee Strengths in the Workplace

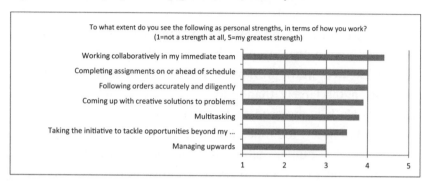

To what extent do you see the following as personal strengths, in terms of how you work?
(1=not a strength at all, 5=my greatest strength)

or relating to others. But it *was* surprising to see how positively people evaluated themselves on some of the specific activities. Most people, for example, thought "working collaboratively in my immediate team" was something they did better than completing assignments on schedule or following orders, despite the fact that effective collaboration is really hard to do and has been shown to be a weakness for many people. Many people said they were good at "coming up with creative solutions," which also flies in the face of evidence for a lack of creativity in large organizations.

So at first glance, these findings suggested the respondents were, at very least, putting a very positive spin on their strengths. They were perhaps focusing on what they would like to be good at, rather than what they were objectively good at. I dug deeper and the story became even more disconcerting. First, I looked for significant variations across companies, age, gender, and so forth, but there were no meaningful patterns. This was very "noisy" data. Next, I compared the ratings these individuals had given themselves and then (for a subsample of 50) I got their own managers to rate them on the same strengths. When I compared the two sets of numbers, I found there was *no significant correlation* between them. In other words, the things the employees said they were good at did not match up with what their managers thought they were good at. It is impossible to say who is right and who is wrong here, but the bottom line is that there is a substantial perception gap when it comes to evaluating employee strengths. This again is a finding that other researchers have confirmed[9].

My simple conclusion from this analysis is *that most of us don't actually know what we are good at.* Partly, this is because we have no solid bases of comparison. Apart from a few activities where there are hard data (e.g. teaching ratings at a university), most of what we do in the workplace is highly open to interpretation. Partly we are also happy to delude ourselves – we talk up our skills in certain desirable areas and we ignore evidence that doesn't fit with our own self-image. As with motivation and fear, the employee's perceptions of his or her strengths are tightly linked to identity.

Career guidance counsellors have known this for years. When mid-career people seek professional advice on what they should do next, it is often because they have a nagging feeling that they have missed their calling in life. However, "calling" is entirely the wrong word. It is rare for someone to have a sufficiently clear sense of what he is good at, and what various careers offer, that he is able to make a straight match. More often, he will jump from job to job, trying each one out for size and looking for the signs that he is getting closer to a good fit. Career counsellors will always ask their clients to evaluate their strengths using the various profiling tools on offer, but they will also use lateral techniques to help their clients know themselves better. When are you at your happiest? When are you most miserable? Who do you envy and why?[10]

As with other aspects of the employee's worldview, managers often have to work pretty hard to divine what their employees' real strengths are. It's not that the employee is being modest or reserved when he doesn't give you a straight answer; more likely, he simply hasn't figured it out himself yet.

I think a significant part of what is happening here that is *many employees haven't taken the time to think actively about these things.* Consider two interviews I conducted during the research. The first was with Harry, a front-line employee in a call center. I asked him to describe his work and what his strengths were. The answer was:

"When customers call, I help them solve their problems. I know the software really well, so I can usually fix their problems pretty quickly. And that's it." I asked about his manager, what he did well, what he could do differently, and the reply was "Well, he is very open, I think, and he does a good job." Harry was a smart guy, no question, but it was clear he hadn't invested any of his intellectual energy in theorizing about his work or about what good management looked like.

The next interview was with Linus, a barman in a hotel. He had just been promoted to head barman, which meant he had a couple of guys reporting to him, and he was responsible for the takings every evening. The same questions led to a much more lively conversation. Linus had a clear view of which parts of the job he was good at, which needed work, and he had a pretty articulate story about his manager's style of working – very direct, no uncertainty about what was needed, but a bit too controlling. In exploring these issues with Linus, it became clear that he had recently made the shift from being managed, which is a passive role, to managing two other people, an active role. He had had to figure out what being a manager meant and this new responsibility suddenly made a lot of his boss' actions more meaningful to him.

What's the bottom line here for you as a manager? Again, some similar themes come out. First, *don't assume your employees have a good sense of their real strengths and weaknesses.* Sure, they will have some views, but they will be a mix of firmly held convictions ("I am hopeless at public speaking") and more lightly held hypotheses ("I think I am a good team player"). It is a worthwhile, though sometimes painful, exercise to compare your evaluations of their strengths against their own, to try to get a better fix on where they should focus their energies in the future.

Second, *it's much easier to be a good employee if you are also someone else's boss.* The beauty of a hierarchical system (except for those right at the bottom or right at the top) is that we are managing up and down at the same time. We can improve the way we manage our employees by learning from the way our boss manages us and we can improve the way we manage our boss by learning from the way we manage our own employees.

SO WHAT DOES AN EMPLOYEE'S EYE-VIEW TELL US?

It can be quite heavy going trying to get inside the heads of your employees, and maybe that is one reason we don't spend much time doing it. There are some pretty obvious points that emerge from this discussion. There are enormous variations in how employees see the world and what their motivations, fears, and strengths are. Their outlook is often very different from that of their managers. Many of them are selling their time for labour, nothing more, and so they haven't invested any emotional energy in understanding the company's wider objectives or plans.

However, there are also some important and surprising insights. Employees often resist what seem to be well-intentioned proposals, and understanding why, in terms of the threat these proposals bring to the employee's self-image, is useful. Making sense of employee fears in terms of Maslow's hierarchy of needs is also potentially quite powerful as a diagnostic device.

Let me summarize the chapter with four observations about your employees:

- *They have an implicit self-identity that shapes their behavior.* Identity is the way people look at themselves. They prefer to take actions that are consistent with and reinforce their identity. They resist initiatives that threaten or impugn that identity.

- *They don't have a great deal of interest in or concern for the company as a whole.* This doesn't mean they are necessarily negative towards the company, but indifference is common. Moreover, such employees often lack the interest to articulate what might make their work more interesting.

- *There is often a lurking cynicism, especially when change programs are introduced.* By cynicism I mean a tendency to frame interventions from above in a negative way. Cynicism ranges from shopfloor banter ("another crazy idea from management") through to poisonous and malicious gossip ("they are only doing this to feather their own nests"). Cynicism is essentially a defence mechanism, and the more often things have gone wrong in the past, the more likely employees are to be wary and guarded next time.

- *Yet despite all this, most employees are not wanting for intellectual or creative skills.* It's just that those skills are being parlayed into opportunities outside their working lives. It is easy to fall into patronizing behavior as a manager, but you do so at your peril.

These characteristics are not uniformly spread across all employees. They are more likely to be seen in certain working environments than others. For example, they are more likely to be true when workers are older, have longer tenure, are unionized, are surrounded by people like themselves, and are operating in a mature industry – Northern Plant and Stitchco being classic examples. They are less likely to be true with a younger and more diverse labor force and in a fast-growing industry where there are lots of opportunities for people to get promoted.

While it is important to understand how your employees look at the world, it is even more important to figure out how to use these insights. In the next chapter, we will turn our attention back to your role as a manager and to the question of how you can help your employees do their best work.

— 4 —

SEEING THE WORLD THROUGH THE EYES OF YOUR EMPLOYEES

You may have seen the hit TV show, Undercover Boss. The Brainchild of UK media executive, Stephen Lambert, the show was launched in the UK in 2009, and has now been rolled out to six other countries. The US series has been enormously popular, with around 18 million regular viewers.

Even if you haven't seen the show, you can probably figure out the storyline. The Chief Executive goes "undercover" for two weeks in his own company, to figure out how things really work. He sees problems that he had not been aware of and he is astounded by the dedication and skills of his workforce. At the end, he reveals who he really is, the employees are shocked, and the CEO resolves to be more open and responsive in the future.

The TV show inevitably focuses on the human interest stories – the wrongly dismissed worker, the single parent working a double shift, the choked-up CEO. But there are also some real management lessons for the Chief Executives who agree to take part. By stepping into the shoes of a front-line worker – and moving out of their comfort zone – for two weeks, they are potentially gaining experiences and insights they simply could not get any other way.

To see what the longer-term consequences of the undercover experience were, I talked to Stephen Martin, CEO of the construction, logistics, and property development company Clugston, and one of the stars of the very first series, broadcast in 2009.

Martin is a modest and reflective man, very keen to do things properly and to make a good impression. His manner is typical of the "quiet" leadership style that came into vogue a few years ago. As he recalls, his initial reaction when the production company asked him to appear in Undercover Boss was no – he did not fancy himself as a TV star. But eventually he came round: "In 2009 we were facing some big challenges, and I am the sort of guy who is always looking for new ideas. So I realized this was an opportunity to make some big changes in how Clugston was working."

Three years on, the experience is still fresh in his mind. "When I did Undercover Boss, I wanted to experience the company from the viewpoint of the workforce. I just found it fascinating to see how everything I thought was working wasn't really working, or if it was, it wasn't working the way I thought it would be. And I also saw the damage I could do, accidentally, by putting in place a new procedure or idea." On one large construction site, for example, it took 10 minutes to walk its length, so workers were spending most of the half-hour tea break travelling to and from the dining area. Martin endorsed a plan to "decentralize" the tea break, so workers could take a break wherever they happened to be working. But somehow this plan got interpreted as the tea break had been cancelled. How is morale? He asked one of his fellow labourers during his time undercover. "At an all-time low" was the response.

Immediately after his undercover stint, Martin made some changes that are still in place three years later. "Seeing things from the front line, I realized how poor we were at communicating. So now we have daily briefings for the direct labour force, weekly meetings with team reps, site notice boards, regular visits from senior managers, and a monthly newsletter, the Clugston Insider. I also introduced skip-level meetings where you discuss things with your boss' boss and brown-bag lunches where I sit down informally with the direct labour force to discuss what is going on. We also brought in a mentoring scheme so that our most experienced workers heading for retirement could pass on their knowledge to the next generation."

Stephen Martin clearly got enormous value from his undercover experience, but when I recount his tale in my seminars, I sometimes get a slightly sceptical reaction. "If he had been doing his job properly in the first place, he wouldn't have needed to go undercover," said one rather grumpy mining company executive.

So there is something a bit puzzling going on here. It is certainly true that a good boss spends time on the front line, getting to know people and exposing him or herself to the day-to-day issues they are facing. But in these situations, he or she is still the boss and they are employees, and the hierarchical nature of this relationship creates an invisible barrier that makes it difficult for employees to be themselves. As Stephen Martin recalls, "When I did site visits as the CEO, I felt people were just telling me what I wanted to hear. When I was working undercover, even with a camera crew following me round, people were incredibly open. It was just a completely different conversation to anything I had heard before."

Martin is describing a well-known phenomenon, the human equivalent of Heisenberg's uncertainty principle (by trying to measure a particle, we disturb it). It is said that the Queen thinks the world smells of fresh paint, as she spends so much time going to grand openings of buildings and sites that have all been spruced up prior to her arrival. To a lesser degree, the same thing happens when you, as an executive, show up on the shopfloor, or even in the pub. You want to know what is going on, but your mere presence changes the dynamics of the conversation. Sometimes the workers may be overly polite and positive; at other times they may pluck up the courage to be critical, but in both cases the message is a "noisy" one that may or may not be representative of what is really happening.

This chapter is all about what you can do as a manager to see the world through your employees' eyes. Most bosses don't have the possibility of going undercover, but of course there are plenty of alternative ways of approximating the undercover experience – getting most of the benefits, but without the same level of investment. I will discuss what some of these are and I will also look at a range of other techniques and concepts to help you reframe the way you look at your organization.

PUTTING YOURSELF IN THEIR SHOES

Before getting into all this, let's briefly take a step back. The notion that you need to see the world through the eyes of others isn't unique to the field of management. The best teachers, for example, have the ability to empathize with their students' learning difficulties. And most professions – from doctors and psychotherapists to solicitors and consultants – have clients whose needs have to be divined and addressed.

In all these professions, the value of the client perspective is recognized but is still very hard to fathom. Consider the case of US surgeon and television personality, Dr Mehmet Oz, who in 2010 had a cancer scare – a couple of precancerous polyps on his colon. While the polyps were caught in time and duly removed, the experience of living through the diagnosis, treatment, and follow-up was a real eye-opener for Dr Oz. It was the first time he had taken the role of patient in the doctor–patient relationship, and the way he behaved took him by surprise. For example, he was meant to go for a check-up 3 months after the initial treatment and he stalled – he scheduled the check-up, then he cancelled, and procrastinated when asked to reschedule. As he recalled, "I was engaging in behaviors that had left me dumbfounded when my patients exhibited them.[1]"

He eventually rescheduled his check-up and was given the all-clear. But why did he stall? Trying to make sense of his behavior after the event, he recounts: ". . . I finally had the epiphany. We are uncomfortable being uncomfortable. We avoid being tested because it creates enormous uncertainty. I have learned to embrace uncertainty. I am pleased that what I learned will help me." The learning here isn't just advice to the people watching his TV show – I think he will also become a better doctor, especially when it comes to helping people take responsibility for going to their scheduled check-ups.

I had an epiphany of my own a couple of years back. In fact it was one of the simple-yet-profound insights that inspired me to write this book[2]. My wife and I were looking to upgrade to a bigger home, so we arranged for the real estate agent to come round and do a valuation of the place where we were living. The day before, my wife suggested we spend a few hours tidying the place up, so that it looked its best. Frankly, I couldn't see the point: surely the real estate agent would be able to figure out what it was worth, regardless of how neat and tidy everything looked? But of course, as a dutiful husband, I went along with the plan anyway, and I did my best to tidy, hoover, plump cushions, and dust. But my heart wasn't in it and my hoovering and dusting skills aren't that strong either. I would clean a room, then my wife would come in after me and clean it again. Soon I found myself checking my Blackberry when my wife was in a different room and deliberately working slowly. Then my mind began to wander and it hit me: this is what it feels like to be an employee. I didn't really understand why I was doing the work and I didn't have the skills to do it well. So I was behaving like a recalcitrant worker – doing the bare minimum to get by, but stalling and idling when given half a chance. I wasn't sabotaging things like the Northern Plant workers in the previous chapter, but I wasn't engaged or motivated either.

The point of the story is the following: for the next couple of weeks, while this learning was still very fresh, I behaved very differently at work. I took much more care with my secretary and my PhD students to clarify what they were doing and why, to structure their work more carefully, and to make sure they had the resources they needed. The adjustments I needed to make were small, but thanks to my home-cleaning experience I took the time to make them.

So why is this sort of mental transposition so powerful in the workplace? I think there are three linked reasons:

- First, and most importantly, *it allows you to understand properly what motivates and concerns the other person.* Dr Oz couldn't figure out why patients would cancel their check-ups until he found himself doing the same thing. I had never understood why there is so much time-wasting in the workplace, until I found myself doing it myself while tidying my home.

- Second, by playing up the view of the other person, *you automatically downplay your own perspective.* In the words of John Lilly, CEO of Mozilla, "When I think in terms of helping people learn to be even better, it automatically puts me into an empathetic mode.[3]" This approach helps you take your own ego and interests out of the equation – an important trait in a good manager.

- Third, putting yourself in the position of the other person *makes you more human in their eyes.* By changing how you relate to your employees, you are likely to see a reciprocal change in behavior on their part as well. Stephen Martin recalls how the Undercover Boss production company came back to his company two years after the original show and there was still a positive buzz across the company. Workers could see that management were trying to make improvements, even if they didn't always work, and to take their views into account.

LESSONS FROM MARKETING

The notion that we should look at the world through someone else's eyes is an old one. Everyday expressions such as exhorting someone "to walk a mile in another's shoes" or to employ someone as a "poacher turned gatekeeper" tap into the same underlying sentiment. However, I think there is some real mileage to be gained by taking the idea seriously, if we can find a way of being systematic about it. Fortunately, there is an enormous body of research and techniques we can make use of in this exercise, namely the field of marketing.

The definition of marketing that has stuck in mind, from when I first studied the subject 20 years ago, is *seeing the world through the eyes of the customer.* If you think about it, the reason we need marketing and marketers is simply that many people fall into the trap of being product-centric: they focus narrowly on the product itself and the clever features it offers, and they neglect the actual needs or concerns of their prospective customers. Companies as different as GM, DEC, Philips, Ericsson, and Kodak have all, to varying degrees, fallen into this trap. Marketers see their job as helping their companies avoid the product-centric trap. Their role is to provide a set of tools, techniques, and frameworks to help companies understand the wants and needs of their prospective customers, and to figure out how to address those needs more effectively.

My simple proposition here is that we can take 60 years' worth of marketing expertise, all focused on developing better ways of seeing the world through the eyes of the customer, and we can apply it to the field of management, which is about seeing the world through the eyes of the employee. This is not a novel idea as such, but applying it systematically to the various elements of management has not been done before.

Figure 4.1 illustrates the overall logic. I have picked out four key themes in the world of marketing and for each one I have identified

Figure 4.1   Applying Marketing Concepts to the Field of Management

MARKETING TOOL	MANAGEMENT INSIGHT
ETHNOGRAPHIC MARKETING Marketers observe how customers behave in real-life, to tap into their unarticulated needs	**CUT THROUGH THE HIERARCHY** Find ways of developing deep and unfiltered insights into how employees view their work
ONE-TO-ONE MARKETING Marketers use technology to tailor their offering around the specific needs of each individual customer	**INDIVIDUALIZED MANAGEMENT** Understand the specific strengths of individual employees, and structure work to play to these strengths
CUSTOMER EXPERIENCE MARKETING Marketers seek to take care of the customer's entire experience with the product or firm	**FOCUS ON EMPLOYEE EXPERIENCE** Build understanding of how employees experience the company, and how it could be improved
NET PROMOTER SCORE Marketers seek to turn their customers into active promoters of their product or service	**TURN EMPLOYEES INTO PROMOTERS** Improve the quality of management so that employees tell their friends and family about it

the analogous theme in the world of management. For each one, we can identify some specific tools and frameworks that can be used directly by managers, to help them understand and relate to their employees more effectively.

A quick note of clarification before proceeding. I make no claim here that I have uncovered some secret new way of managing employees; all the concepts I describe here can be found somewhere in the Human Resource Management literature. However, sometimes a new angle on an old problem is useful. A change in perspective, as they say, is worth 50 IQ points. Hopefully, by looking at these challenges through a different frame, you will see opportunities for managing your employees a little differently.

CUT THROUGH THE HIERARCHY TO BUILD EMPLOYEE INSIGHT

An important technique in the field of marketing is *ethnography* – the study of customer behavior in its naturally occurring context. Academic research in marketing has used ethnography since the 1970s, but over the last 15 years or so the technique has been increasingly adopted by professional marketers as well.

Marketers have embraced ethnography because there is only so much insight you can get from a focus group, survey, or taste test. We know that customers often don't behave the way they say they will (New Coke was a hit on paper and a disaster in practice), and we know that customers struggle to articulate their unmet needs (Henry Ford's customers reputedly wanted a faster horse). So increasingly, marketers have figured out that you get real insight only by "living with" customers in their natural habitat – following them round the supermarket, watching them cook dinner, and observing them as they struggle to get their kids to try new foods. Good ethnography yields insights about customers that they themselves are unaware of. Procter & Gamble's Swiffer cleaner, for example, was invented when Harry West, a leader on the soap team, observed a woman wipe the floor with a paper towel[4]. He didn't ask her how to improve the traditional mop, but by watching her in her natural setting he was able to make the creative leap that resulted in the Swiffer – a product that became a $500m per year revenue earner for the company.

How can we apply the marketing concept of ethnography to the practice of management? Well, hopefully the answer is pretty obvious. We saw in Chapter 3 that employees have a self-identity, a view of themselves that they seek to reinforce through their behavior. But they often struggle to articulate what this identity is. Their knowledge about themselves is tacit – they know more than they can tell. So just as ethnographers seek to divine insights from customers about their latent needs by observing them, good managers seek to generate an understanding of their employees, by picking up cues about what engages them and what turns them off.

Ethnography is also a way of breaking down barriers. People can be very defensive when asked straight market research questions, so ethnographers work hard to put their subjects at ease and to gradually build their trust. Equally, as we saw at the beginning of the chapter, employees are always on their guard when the boss is in the room, for fear of saying something wrong or letting information slip. So the boss has to find creative ways of overcoming their defensive behavior.

An ethnographic approach to management actually looks a lot like what Stephen Martin did for two weeks as an undercover boss. While he didn't use this term, the principles are exactly the same: he observed his employees in their natural environment, without "disturbance" from top management, and he got them to articulate their views about how things were going.

I appreciate that it isn't too practical for you to put yourself on an undercover assignment, so we have to think creatively about alternative approaches that go some way towards providing the deep insights into our employees that we need. Here is a list of some of the approaches I have seen:

- Institutionalized "skip-level" meetings. Skip level simply means meeting with people two levels above (or below) you in the hierarchy. Some companies have a strong informal norm that you don't break the chain of command. This norm helps to build accountability, but at the same time it restricts the flow of information. Stephen Martin realized this was happening at Clugston, so he introduced skip-level meetings as a way of getting senior executives more involved in the day-to-day realities of the business. By scheduling them regularly – every two months – they simply became a standard part of the manager's job. Martin also introduced informal "brown bag" lunches with employees to serve a similar function.

- Web-enabled chat and discussion forums. In large companies, it is simply impossible for all employees to meet their top executives. However, technology provides a mechanism to give people at least a virtual connection to the top. For example, the Indian IT Services company, HCL Technologies, has a tool on its Intranet called *You & I*, where the CEO gives direct answers to questions posed by employees. A voting system is used to prioritize the questions and then, once a week, Nayar sits down for a couple of hours and writes answers to the questions at the top of the list. Many companies have also been experimenting with microblogging tools such as Yammer (recently bought by Microsoft). Microblogging allows employees to sign up to conversation threads about topics of interest to them, and it encourages informal, nonhierarchical discussions. At CapGemini, for example, Yammer has become an important tool. As explained by former Chief Technology Officer, Andy Mulholland, it provides "vital insight into what's going on across our business" while also providing "social glue" for the 20 000 employees who have signed up to it (I will discuss this case in more detail in Chapter 7).

- Executives doing front-line work. This is the simplest and best-known way of cutting through the hierarchy. For example, executives at Tesco, the biggest UK supermarket chain, spend one week every year working in the stores – on the checkout desk, behind the fish counter, stacking the shelves. While this isn't undercover work – everyone knows the grey-haired guy behind the counter is the CEO – it still serves to remind executives of the day-to-day issues their employees have to deal with, and it makes them look a lot more human as well. There are even some industries where executives see front-line work as part of their job. The Managing Director of a John Lewis store, for example, will spend an hour or two every day on the floor, serving customers alongside his staff. In my world, many business school Deans still find the time to teach the occasional MBA course.

- Smokers' corner. These days, smokers find themselves driven out into the parking lot, or on to the streets outside their office building, to indulge their craving for nicotine. The one silver lining for these marginalized individuals is that they often find themselves chatting to people they wouldn't otherwise bump into, while having their cigarette. This is the sort of forum where gossip is shared, and perhaps because the relationship is smoker to smoker, rather than employee to boss, the usual hierarchical barriers seem to be suspended. I have often heard senior executives comment that they pick up on the "pulse" of the company more in their 15-minute cigarette breaks than they do in any number of formal meetings.

  Of course, taking up smoking as a way of finding out what is happening in the company would be a rather drastic step to take, but there are other pursuits that also cut across the usual barriers. I know senior executives who are members of the squash and running clubs in their organizations, and these also provide a nonhierarchical window on what is going on.

- Reverse mentoring. A traditional mentoring relationship is a way for a seasoned professional to share wisdom with a more junior person who is still learning the ropes. However, the speed of change in the world of technology has given rise to the concept of reverse mentoring, in which a young, tech-savvy employee helps an older manager to get up to speed in the latest developments in technology. When it works well, this form of reverse mentoring can be a great opportunity for both parties. For example, one of the people I interviewed for this book is Ross Smith, a late-forties executive at Microsoft. He is being mentored by a 28 year old, to keep him up to date on new social media applications and to get him into the mindset of so-called "Gen Y" employees. Unlike traditional mentoring, this ends up as a two-way relationship, and they end up discussing a wide range of issues on a much more informal basis than would be possible usually.

This is not meant to be a comprehensive list. There are many traditional techniques that I have not talked about – from town hall meetings to "Management by Walking Around" – that all help you cut through the hierarchy to various degrees. For you as a manager, the trick is to choose something that fits your own style of working, so that your employees recognize it as an authentic attempt to understand their point of view.

INDIVIDUALIZING THE EMPLOYEE PROPOSITION

In the field of marketing, there has been a significant evolution in thinking about how to address customer needs. In the early days of marketing, adverts on TV, radio, and billboards were a form of *mass marketing*, with all potential customers receiving the same message. This one-size-fits-all approach gradually gave way to *market segmentation*, with subgroups of potential customers being identified and targeted with different offerings. The trend nowadays is towards *one-to-one marketing* or *mass customization*, in which the offering is tailored to the specific needs of the prospective customer. Examples include Amazon sending you personalized recommendations on the basis of your previous purchases, Yahoo! allowing you to specify the various elements of your home page, and Dell letting you configure the various components of your computer before it is assembled. These offerings have been enabled by technological innovation. While one-to-one marketing used to be feasible only for very high-end customers, advances in flexible manufacturing and online analytical techniques have brought the potential of customization to the masses.

How can we apply the principle of one-to-one marketing to the practice of management? Again, the basic intuition here should be pretty clear. In the industrial era, manufacturing companies employed people primarily to do manual labour and one worker was much like the next. As Henry Ford famously said: "Why is it that whenever I ask for a pair of hands, a brain comes attached?" But in today's knowledge economy, most employees are hired for their brains, not their hands. This makes for a far more heterogeneous workforce, where all workers have their own unique skills and capabilities. What workers want, in other words, is jobs that are customized to their needs.

Unfortunately, most companies are still stuck in an industrial era mindset. Most low-end jobs are designed so that individual workers can be swapped in and out at minimal cost (e.g., hamburger flipping or telephone sales). Even in higher-end work, it is still standard practice to define generic jobs that any qualified employees can slot themselves into. According to this model, employees are expected to adjust themselves to the roles they are assigned, rather than the other way around. In the language of marketing, jobs are still for the most part "off-the-rack" rather than "made-to-measure" creations.

The management challenge for companies is to see how far the principles of one-to-one marketing can be applied to the employee relationship. Conceptually, this means *individualizing the employee proposition*, that is, creating a better match between the demands of the job and the capabilities of the employee. As usual, this is an idea that has been around for a while. Marcus Buckingham's work on strengths, described in Chapter 3, builds on this premise, as does Chris Bartlett and Sumantra Ghoshal's book *The Individualized Corporation*. Some of Peter Drucker's work also anticipated this trend: "The goal [of management]," he wrote, "is to make productive the specific strengths and knowledge of each individual.[5]"

Let's be clear: designing work around employees, rather than vice versa, is a costly business. Just as in marketing, we need to balance the company's need for efficiency and standardization with the employee's need for a "tailored" job that matches unique skills. Particularly in industries where talent is scarce, there is a lot of scope for putting more emphasis on tailoring the job to the individual, because that is what will encourage employees to stick around. As in the field of marketing, new technologies are making it possible to shift the trade-off, to get the best of both worlds. Here are a few examples of what I am talking about:

- HCL Technologies, the Indian IT services company, has developed a tool called "Employee Passion Indicative Count" (EPIC), which I described briefly in Chapter 3. EPIC is a survey employees fill in to indicate how excited they are about various aspects of their work – who they are as individuals, what work they like to do and where, and who they like to work with. At an aggregate level, this survey provides the company with important insights into what motivates their workers: for example, in 2010 the top passion indicator for male employees was "customer support" whereas for female employees it was "collaboration." EPIC also works as a management tool. "Each line manager reviews his employees' EPIC scores," explains Anand Pillai, former head of talent management at HCL, "and this opens up a conversation about what sort of work he should be doing. We discovered some employees wanted to do customer-facing work, while others showed a preference for back-office activities like testing software and doing documentation. In many cases, we are able to move people to jobs they are more excited about. In cases where we cannot make the match immediately, we help them build the competencies they need to move.[6]"

- Ross Smith is Director of the 85-person Lync Test team at Microsoft and an ardent believer in the employee-centric approach to management. When Microsoft Lync 2010 was released, preparation for the next version began. Smith realized that a reorganization of the team would be needed, but he knew how disruptive and demotivating such changes can be. So he and his team decided to experiment with a bottom-up process that the entire team would be involved in, what they dubbed a "we-org". Rather than asking his four direct reporters to pick their teams, they asked individual contributors to select which teams they would like to be in. As explained by Dan Bean, one of Smith's management team, these individuals "became free agents, looking for an optimal position, much like a sports star.'" The four managers were not in a position to offer more money to these free agents, but they could offer them opportunities for growth, new technologies to work on, and new colleagues to work with. The individual contributors quickly warmed to this new process. "The initial feeling was, oh, it's a reorg again, nobody was excited that it was happening. But after the meeting [with Ross Smith], it became clear they were really serious about accommodating everyone's choices. The next couple of days we saw marked changes. Now it was about what have you decided? rather than what did you get?" The we-org took longer than anticipated, but the bottom line was that 95% of the team liked or somewhat liked the new method, and only two individuals out of 85 felt that they did not end up with a satisfactory placement in the new structure.

- AdNovum is a Zurich-based software company founded by Stefan Arn. Around 2002, the company had grown to around 30 people and Arn realized he needed to build some sort of system for matching his employees to projects. In his market for security software, flexibility was also important. "So we developed a Facebook-like system on the Web where you as an employee could portray yourself, especially your skill set, for others to review," he recalled, "and we encouraged people to keep their CVs and their skill sets as accurate as possible." Very quickly, the new system became something of a competition: people could apply for a project by looking at the pipeline of new projects and deciding which ones suited their skills and preferences, while at the same time project heads were calling up the people they wanted. Using the data on how many times developers were asked for by projects, Arn developed a performance-based ranking, which he then posted on the

Intranet for all to see. He also linked the individual's position in the ranking system with their bonus[8].

While these three examples differ on many points, the common principle is clear: give employees more choice over what they do. At HCL, EPIC is about helping employees to articulate what they are passionate about and building these preferences into their development plan. At Microsoft, the we-org was about letting employees choose their role in the new structure. At AdNovum, the system Stefan Arn created allowed people to apply for specific projects, according to their skills and motivations.

Are we seeing a trend towards the employee equivalent of one-to-one marketing? Well, there are plenty of companies experimenting with this type of approach, but the management effort required in structuring work around the needs of individual employees is substantial. Ross Smith's we-org was a success, but perhaps only because he had already established a high level of trust within the team for his unconventional approach to management. While AdNovum's market-based model for matching people and projects worked well while the company was small, as it has grown it has gradually adopted a hybrid project–management system, using much more of the traditional top-down approach. There is a tension, in other words, between the broader demands of the organization and the specific needs of the employee, and an important part of the manager's job is to get the right balance between these two opposing forces.

MANAGING THE EMPLOYEE EXPERIENCE

One of the big trends in the field of marketing over the last 20 years has been an increasing focus on the *customer experience*. It is argued that increasingly customers are buying an experience, not a product or service. That is why we are prepared to pay $4 for a coffee at Starbucks – we are buying a pleasant coffee-drinking experience with comfy chairs and jazz music, rather than a cup of hot caffeinated liquid.

To turn this broad idea into something practical, marketers have sought to understand why some companies – Apple, Porsche, Virgin Atlantic – are able to generate consistently positive views about how people experience their product or service, while their competitors are not. Certainly there are intangible aspects of the brand at play here, but of far greater importance are the "touch points" where the customer or potential customer interacts directly with the product or the company. The legendary CEO of Scandinavian Airlines (SAS), Jan Carlzon, called these the *moments of truth*. Your experience as an airline passenger, he argued, is defined more by how you are treated at check-in, at the gate, or on board the aircraft, than it is by the actual food you are served or the route you flew.

As always, there are several different marketing tools out there to help companies manage their customer experience. One is Customer Experience Management, defined as "the process of strategically managing a customer's entire experience with a product or company[9]"; another is the Service Profit Chain, which is about defining and managing the sequence of activities that drive customer satisfaction and loyalty in service industries (e.g., airlines, banks, retailers). The common theme, for our purposes here, is simply that customers develop a perception of the product or company largely through human interaction. The technical qualities of a product matter, but the way the product is experienced is more important.

How can we apply these marketing insights to the practice of management? Employees, like customers, enter a relationship with a company that they can exit at any time. However, it is in the interests of the company to retain both its customers and employees. There is solid evidence that loyal customers drive long-term profitability. There is equally solid evidence that low turnover and talent retention are key dimensions of organizational health.

So what are the factors that explain employee turnover? Salary is obviously part of the story, but actually a surprisingly small part. There are also long-term factors, in terms of whether employees find the work engaging and whether the company gives the individual opportunities to develop. Many employees quit before these issues even begin to surface. Some industries have employee turnover rates above 50% per year. In these high-turnover industries – hotels, restaurants, call centers – a particular problem is people quitting within a couple of months of starting.

It is this early-stage turnover that the research on customer experience can really help. I believe companies can do a much better job of managing the employee experience. This includes the various touch points the employee has with people in the company, especially in the first few months, as well as the physical working environment and the day-to-day routine of work. If this initial experience is poor, the employee gets a bad initial impression and often will not wait to find out if things could improve.

Increasingly, companies are looking for thoughtful ways of managing the employee experience. Consider two examples from sectors where employee turnover rates are typically very high:

- [24]7 Inc., headquartered in Campbell, California, provides innovative customer service solutions to its clients. Most of its 10 000 employees work in service centers in India, Philippines, and Guatemala, and employee turnover rates in these cities is often as high as 100% per year. The company's co-founder and Chief People Officer, Shanmugam Nagarajan (Nags), explained how he keeps turnover rates down to about half the industry average. "I spend about a quarter of my time on the road, meeting with around 500 front-line employees every quarter, listening to their concerns and following up with fixes. Transparency and accessibility are key values in the company. We have also put in place what we call '90 day surveys.' Our analysis showed that if new employees make it through the first 90 days, they are likely to stick around. So we focus a lot on those first touch points when a new employee starts, and we survey them. Are you satisfied with the office? The food? The transportation to work? Do you have the support you need? Often we can make small changes as a result of these surveys, and that creates a positive experience that encourages employees to stay. For people who have been with us a while we also have a training program, 'Wings Within,' for helping employees to make internal transfers into different functional areas.[10]"

- HCL Technologies has what it calls a "Smart Service Desk" (SSD) for its employees. This concept was borrowed directly from the world of marketing. Many companies use service tickets as a way of monitoring and following up on customer complaints. Vineet Nayar, former CEO of HCL Technologies (now Vice Chair), had the bright idea of applying this approach inside the company. As he explains, "Value is created by employees in their relationship with customers. So management's job is to serve the employees. The Smart Service Desk is one of several tools we have created to help management serve the employees better." As an employee at HCL, if you are unhappy about some aspect of your work, or need a problem resolving, you open a Service Ticket with the relevant manager, perhaps the head of human resources or the facilities manager in your office. It is up to that person to resolve the problem and the ticket is only closed when the employee is satisfied. This IT-enabled system keeps track of the number of tickets being opened and how quickly they are closed. Unresolved tickets are then escalated to higher levels in the company. The SSD concept puts the onus on managers to become more service-oriented, so that employees feel they are getting a good experience.

These two examples are based on low-end jobs in the high-turnover IT sector, largely because the challenges are so acute here. Clearly the concept of improving the employee experience applies much more broadly as well. There is room for considerable creativity here, in dreaming up novel ways of enriching your employees' experiences in the workplace.

TURNING EMPLOYEES INTO ADVOCATES

Finally, an important theme in marketing over the last decade has been the idea that the best advocates of a company or its brand are its own customers. It has always been true that word-of-mouth promotion is the most powerful endorsement you can receive for your product. In the online world, the power of customers-as-advocates has increased dramatically: a favorable review, tweet, or blog from someone who raves about your product can quickly reach thousands of potential customers. The reverse is also true: a disaffected customer can make your life miserable very quickly. In 2009, musician Dave Carroll posted his song "United [Airlines] Breaks Guitars" on YouTube and within four days the company's share price had dropped 10%.

Fred Reichheld, author of *The Loyalty Effect* and *The Ultimate Question*, has pushed this concept of customers as advocates furthest through his development of the "Net Promoter Score" (NPS), which is based on answers to the question "How likely is it that you would recommend our company to a friend or colleague?" By taking the "promoters" (who give a score of 9 or 10 out of 10) and subtracting the "detractors" (who give a score of 6 or lower out of 10), you end up with a single net score (a percentage of the total number of respondents), which indicates how much customers are talking positively about your company. Many large companies use the NPS as a key performance indicator, and it has been shown to be highly correlated with long-term performance[11].

How can we use this concept to help improve the practice of management? Clearly, it makes sense that we want our employees to be positive advocates of our company. Engaged employees are likely to talk up the company and its products to their friends, which in turn is good for sales and for attracting new employees.

We can go further. Reichheld's research makes the point that you don't just want satisfied customers, you want customers who are sufficiently "wowed" that they say it is "extremely likely" they will recommend you to a friend or colleague. These are the ones that make a real difference, the ones who make "viral" marketing happen. I think the same is true of your employees. Of course you want happy and engaged people working in your company, but it's the highly engaged ones that make a real difference, because their enthusiasm is infectious.

In 2010, I was working with a team from the Swiss pharmaceutical company, Roche, who had the bright idea of applying the Net Promoter Score internally. They developed their own metric, which they called the Net Management Promoter Score (NMPS). The question was worded as follows:

How likely is it that you would recommend your line manager to a colleague, as someone they should work for in the future (1 = not at all, 10 = extremely likely)?

The team's thinking was that this question would be a useful way of getting a grip on the overall quality of management in the company. They really liked how sharp and to-the-point it was. "I have often filled in pages and pages of questions in 360-degree feedback surveys about people in my organization, and after a while you lose focus," recalled Jesper Ek, one member of the team. "If we could narrow down to a single, meaningful measure, everyone would benefit.[12]"

The team trialled the NMPS with a subgroup of managers and they showed that it was strongly correlated to Roche's broader measures of employee engagement. The results were presented to various senior executives, two of whom quickly incorporated the measure into their own quarterly employee survey. "I would like to see it used to compare the performances of different regions or business units, over time," said Jesper Ek. "An improving aggregated score year-on-year would be a great advert for prospective employees. NMPS could even be used as a means of comparing the performance of our own business with that of a competitor. There is huge scope to expand the concept."

Following the success of this Roche experiment, I have also used the NMPS in some of my research. I think it potentially serves two purposes. First, it is a useful overall indicator of the quality of management in a unit or organization. For example, in the survey I described in Chapter 3, the NMPS ranged from −28% in one company through to +61% in another. In the lowest one, there were 28% more people who were detractors than promoters of their managers and in the highest there were 61% more promoters than detractors. This compared with an overall measure (for the sample as a whole) of −15%. By tracking this number over time, you get an interesting indicator of how well managed a company is.

The NMPS could also potentially be used as feedback for individual managers, as one indicator of how good a job they are doing. It's worth underlining that Fred Reichheld's research showed that a score of 6 out of 10 (or below) is negative and it is only a score of 9 or 10 out of 10 that really counts as a positive endorsement. This means that many managers end up with more "detractors" than "promoters" – this is tough feedback, but ultimately very useful if you want to create an organization where your employees can do their best work.

I plotted the NMPS against an established measure of employee engagement and the results (see Figure 4.2) suggested a very strong correlation of 0.75. Remember, employee engagement is an indicator of how much discretionary effort a person is likely to put into their job and it is influenced by a range of factors, including the nature of the work itself, the physical working environment, the opportunities for development, and the quality of colleagues. This chart simply says that all these other factors are secondary – it is the quality of your

Figure 4.2 Employee Engagement and the Net Management Promoter Score

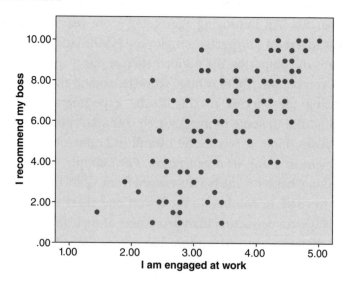

immediate boss that has the biggest single impact on your overall engagement at work.

THINKING LIKE A MARKETER

In this chapter, I have shown how you can apply your employee's eye-view to the work of management. As always, the challenge is moving from concept to practice, which is why the techniques from the world of marketing are so useful. Marketers have developed an impressive toolkit to help them tap into and address their customers' needs, and quite a few of their tools are immediately applicable to the world of management.

Indeed, I am sure there are other marketing techniques that could have potentially been discussed here. I encourage you to think creatively about all the different approaches you can use to get closer to your customers and to see if those principles could also help you become a better manager.

— 5 —

DOING WHAT WE KNOW WE SHOULD: MANAGING AS AN UNNATURAL ACT

If you want to make improvements to the practice of management, start in your own backyard. This was the view of a team of executives at If, the leading Scandinavian insurance company. As part of a strategic review, they had become aware of the untapped talent of many front-line employees, and they developed the simple hypothesis that this potential might be opened up with a more supportive and coaching-oriented style of management. "We thought that by acting in a slightly different way, and emphasizing intrinsic rather than extrinsic motivation, our managers might make a real difference to the competence and performance of our employees," recalls Hakan Johansson, one of the executives[1].

So here is what they did. They identified a team in Johansson's division – an already high-performing team selling insurance for cars by phone – and they persuaded the team leader, Lotta Laitinen, to make some changes to her management style. Lotta was excused from two hours a day of meetings and routine admin (which were handled by an obliging colleague), time which instead she would spend directly with her team, both jointly and individually.

The process was kicked off with a workshop, introduced by Johansson, in which Lotta's team was asked to discuss the value of cross-selling, and how it might be improved. "This was the starting point for it, to give more influence to the team," noted Niclas Ward, one of Johansson's colleagues. Following this workshop, Lotta, with her extra two hours a day, began working much more closely with the team, working with the high performers to understand the tricks of their trade, listening to sales calls, and coaching members of the team on a one-to-one basis. Team members were also encouraged to listen to and coach each other, with Lotta also joining in and giving feedback.

After three weeks of the new way of working, the results were measured in three ways – by actual performance, through a questionnaire completed by the whole group, and by selective interviews. The headline figure was a 5% increase in sales, compared to the three previous weeks. The overall figure concealed some unanticipated differences: notably, there were major improvements among the hitherto below-average performers. The questionnaire responses were uniformly positive, team members strongly agreeing that the approach was indeed different, that they had more freedom to work in the way that suited them, that they got more time with the leader, and that they felt more motivated. The highest score was recorded by the proposition "I would like to work the way we worked in the last three weeks in the future." Lotta's reaction was also positive, initial hesitancy giving way to strong enthusiasm as the trial went on and she continued to find fresh ways to work. She was adamant that she missed nothing by not going to the meetings. "The first week was really stressful, because I had to make plans for the three weeks," she summed up. "But by the middle of the test period, I was more relaxed, and I was satisfied when I went home every day because I felt I had had a great day."

So were the If executives happy with this outcome? Absolutely. A 5% boost in sales over three weeks is impressive and bringing up the performance of the weaker members of the team was a real plus. The cost of the intervention was minimal – Lotta was confident she could continue to carve out more time for coaching, even without the help of an obliging colleague, by simply becoming more efficient in her administrative tasks. At the time of writing, Johansson and his colleagues were looking to scale this initiative up: "We are now developing specific plans for how to help our front-line managers across the organization become more effective coaches, and how to free up some of their time so they do more of the real value-added parts of their job. There is a big payoff to the company if we can get this right."

Here is the real point of this story. Just like Google's advice on how to become a better manager (mentioned in the introduction), the notion that coaching your employees might help their performance is obvious. *All it took was a simple and deliberate intervention from Hakan Johansson and his colleagues for a worthwhile change in behavior to occur.* Why had this change not happened earlier? I don't believe Lotta was at fault – in fact she was chosen for the task because she was competent, personable, and open to new ways of thinking. However, like so many other managers in companies around the world, she was so busy with tedious administrative jobs that she wasn't making the time to do the potentially more valuable parts of her job.

DOING WHAT WE KNOW WE SHOULD

This chapter is about how you can do your job as a manager more effectively – how you can become a better boss. In the previous chapter, the focus was on knowing your employees better and seeing the world through their eyes. In this chapter, the focus is on *knowing yourself better*. As managers, we like to think we are doing a good job but, if we are being truthful with ourselves, we know there are things we could do better, especially in terms of how we get the most out of our employees. Just flip back to the list at the end of Chapter 2: what employees want is challenging work, space, support, and recognition. Do *you* consistently provide these things to all your employees? My guess is sometimes you do, but at other times you lapse back into less desirable behaviors such as micromanaging, selfishness, or inattentiveness.

Why don't we do what we know we should? Again, Chapter 2 provided the simplistic answers: we are too busy, we have conflicting priorities, and our employees have such different needs that it is hard to keep them all happy. But there is much more going on here as well. This so-called "knowing–doing" gap is a pervasive problem, even with managers who have plenty of time and few direct reports.

I think there are two linked explanations for the knowing–doing gap in managers. One is that many managers don't truly, deeply believe in the importance of giving their employees lots of space, or coaching them, or providing proper feedback. Seasoned managers develop a point of view based on their personal experience, and this typically trumps any sort of research-based findings as a guide for action. So even if a manager accepts – intellectually – the findings about what might make him or her more effective, he or she will often quite happily act in a contrary way, just based on personal experience.

The other explanation is that we don't turn knowledge into action. Using the terminology popularized by Chip and Dan Heath in their best-seller *Switch*, the rational part of our mind, the "Rider," has figured out the path to take, but the emotional part, the "Elephant," isn't moving. Just like losing weight or exercising more, there are aspects of good management that we know we should do, but other things just keep on getting in the way. We lack the self-control to do what we know we should.

In this chapter, we discuss these arguments in detail and we lay out a way forward. To become a better manager, you need to develop self-awareness, so that you are more conscious of the less-than-rational ways you often behave. Armed with these insights, you can then develop a set of techniques and tricks to help you change your behavior. This chapter will highlight what some of these tricks are. Changing your own behavior is not easy, but it is possible, and the rewards – for you and for your team – are substantial.

WHY DO WE BEHAVE THE WAY WE DO?

There is mounting evidence that we are all behaviorally flawed. We have biases and shortcomings in the way we process information and how we act on it. These biases detract from our ability to take the rational or smart course of action in a particular situation.

Psychologists have been studying these behavioral flaws for a very long time, but over the last decade or so the world of mainstream economics has belatedly come to realize that these apparently small deviations from their rational theories of human nature actually have profound consequences for decision-making, human interaction, and life in general. The field of *behavioral economics* is now growing rapidly and its findings are influencing corporate boardrooms and government policymakers alike.

Behavioral economics attempts to make sense of the weird and wonderful ways the human brain works. Daniel Kahneman, Nobel Laureate and founding father of this field of research, says that problems stem from the fact that we have two parallel systems in our minds:

- System 1 operates automatically, with little or no effort. We can detect hostility in a voice, drive a car on an empty road, or understand simple sentences, without any sense of voluntary control.

- System 2 requires the conscious allocation of mental effort. If we want to check the validity of a logical argument, monitor the appropriateness of our behavior in a social situation, or tell someone our phone number, we have to pay careful attention to the task in hand[2].

These two parallel systems have been characterized in many different ways: the doer and the planner; the emotional and the rational; the id and the superego; and the elephant and the rider. Very often, our behavioral flaws occur because System 1 (the elephant) has already reacted to a situation before System 2 (the rider) has had a chance to intervene. This is why we procrastinate, why we make snap decisions that are wrong, and why we occasionally get into fights. Sometimes, though, the problem is the other way round and System 2 takes over, leading us to overanalyse a problem or become overwhelmed by the choices we face.

Why do our brains work this way? There isn't complete agreement, but one influential line of thinking called *evolutionary psychology* says that the minds and bodies of humans are, in large part, adapted to the demands of their ancestral environment – the "social clan life of mobile hunter-gatherers" that was still the dominant way of life until around 10 000 years ago[3]. In essence, this theory says the human mind is evolving over time, but it is struggling to keep up with the speed of changes in human civilization, so we end up with mismatches between our "natural" response to a situation (i.e., how our ancestors would have responded) and the "appropriate" response (i.e., what works best in a modern context). This is why we prefer to work in small teams, not in large impersonal organizations; why we make risky bets when faced with the prospect of loss; and why we react violently when we feel threatened, even if we put ourselves in danger in the process.

While I found these arguments pretty persuasive, I realize that many people find it a bit of a stretch to link the actions of hunter-gatherers on the savannah to modern day human behavior. So be it. For our purposes here, it is much less important to worry about the origins of our behavioral flaws than to recognize how and where they manifest themselves. We need to be conscious of our own biases and shortfalls, so that we can take the appropriate remedial actions.

So here is the key idea in this chapter. For the majority of us, *management is an unnatural act*[4]. We know what good management looks like, but it takes a lot of conscious effort to follow through on it. Using Kahneman's terminology, our System 1 response as a manager is often very different to what our System 2 logic would tell us we should do, so we have to work extra hard to do what we know we should. Using the logic of evolutionary psychology, the reason good management is so difficult is that our natural predisposition is towards what worked in our ancestral environment – which was about hunting and foraging in small tribes, not coordinating large, diversified organizations.

Fortunately, our conscious mind is able to get to grips with this dilemma. In the words of management writer David Hurst, our true nature is "an ancient selfishness overlaid with a profound ability to cooperate and varnished with a thin layer of reason.[5]" It is this thin layer of reason, part of Kahneman's System 2, that I am appealing to

Figure 5.1   The Three Basic Principles of Good Management

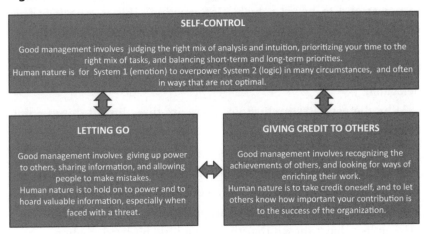

here, so that you as an individual can find ways of making the unnatural act of managing a little more natural.

To provide some structure to the rest of this chapter, I think it is useful to break good management down into two linked sets of principles: *letting go*, which means giving up power to others, sharing information, and letting people make mistakes; and *giving credit to others*, which means recognizing their achievements and looking for ways to enrich their work. Sitting above these two sets of principles is a third principle we can call *self-control*, which means making the right trade-offs and choices among competing alternatives. Figure 5.1 illustrates how these three principles fit together.

LETTING GO: WHY IS IT DIFFICULT?

One of the hallmarks of a good manager is the capacity to let go – to give power and freedom to others, to share information freely and willingly, and to allow people to make mistakes. We know from Chapter 2 this is what our employees want us to do and we know from Chapter 1 that a people-centric culture based on empowerment and shared information drives long-term success.

But letting go is difficult to do. It is human nature to hold on to power and to hoard valuable information. This is especially true when things are not going well: if your organization is under threat, you are likely to be become more controlling, by asking for more frequent reports and checking details that you would normally have delegated.

Why the gap? Research shows there are three linked things going on here:

1. *The principle of loss aversion.* As individuals, we work hard to avoid a loss and we are more concerned about avoiding a loss than making a gain. For example, studies of professional golfers have shown that they try a little bit harder when putting to save par than when putting for a birdie. Studies of court cases have shown that people will accept a significantly lower settlement than they deserve to avoid the small risk of losing a case. In other words, there is a simple but profound asymmetry between how we behave when facing upside opportunity and downside risk. Averting financial loss, and also loss-of-face to others, is a strong driver of behavior.

2. *The illusion of control.* We like to believe ourselves to be in control of the events that shape our lives. It has been shown, for example, that people who have been involved in failures seek to reassure themselves that they have learnt from their mistakes, even when the failures were evidently not their fault. We are also apt to observe causality and intentionality in entirely random events, because our brains are wired to seek out patterns.

3. *The knowledge is power syndrome.* From Rupert Murdoch to Kim Jong Il, the ability to control the flow of information has long been recognized as a key source of power. At a much more modest level, many managers use their privileged access to personnel reports or company accounts to justify and sustain their position. We know that the scarcity of a resource such as knowledge makes it appear more valuable. We also

know that once someone "owns" a piece of information, they place a value on it rather greater than they would if they had to acquire it. There are many reasons for withholding, rather than sharing, important information in an organizational setting.

Put these three drivers together and you can quickly see how they lead to suboptimal management behavior. The principle of loss aversion encourages managers to work extra hard in a tough market to ensure they deliver on their promises, which almost always involves more oversight of subordinates. The illusion of control reinforces managers' belief that their involvement is critical to the outcome of a decision. The knowledge-is-power syndrome also encourages managers to keep information to themselves, typically under the delusional belief that it is confidential.

I have personal experience of how this plays out. A few years ago, I was involved in launching a new product that various stakeholders didn't like. My role was to work up the business plan, think through the specific details of the product, and to assuage the concerns of the unhappy stakeholders. During one critical period before launch, I was working 10 hours a day on the project, often negotiating with several stakeholders simultaneously. What I needed to do my job was the freedom to make my own decisions and to communicate swiftly. However, my boss was also feeling the heat from *his* stakeholders, so he responded by reining me in, second-guessing some of my decisions, and micromanaging my communications. This of course made things worse, as we wasted a lot of time arguing about the best course of action rather than just getting things done.

Here is another example. Many companies over the last decade have introduced the notion of a "performance contract" between a business unit and corporate headquarters, as a way of specifying *what* has to be delivered, but leaving lots of discretion to the business unit managers in terms of *how* it will be done. In theory it is a good way of pushing decision-making closer to the action and empowering business unit managers. In practice, though, the performance contract has often become an insidious device for achieving the exact opposite outcome.

I was talking to a senior executive in one of the big five UK banks and he explained how their performance contract had gradually grown in length, from a focus on 4–5 measures to a list of more than 15 different measures. "I have so many things I am now accountable for," he explained, "that I have lost most of my managerial discretion. There are just too many things I am being measured against. The performance contract has turned into a big stick – something to beat me over the head with."

LETTING GO: SOME ADVICE ON DOING IT BETTER

So what can you do to be more effective and more consistent in letting go? The starting point, as always, is to get it clear in your own head why giving your employees freedom is the right approach. Everyone has their own way of doing this and you have to try a number of different angles before finding the one that resonates best. A friend of mine, Andrew Dyckhoff, is an executive coach, and he expresses it in the following way: "I ask the person I am coaching, do you hold yourself to higher standards than those around hold you to? Yes, they invariably reply. So I ask the supplementary question: so why would your employees, the people who work for you, not do the same?" By exposing this implicit double standard, Andrew helps the executive to think more carefully about the amount of trust he has in those around him.

A related approach is to be more honest about what is holding you back from delegating and sharing more with your employees. In one recent piece of research I was involved in, we asked managers to assess (a) how important and (b) how easy to delegate their various day-to-day activities were. Perhaps unsurprisingly, they said the least important activities were also the most easy to delegate. Which begged the question, why on earth were they not delegating these things? On further inspection, it became clear that many of these activities were things the managers got some sort of tacit utility out of – departmental meetings where they had an opportunity to banter and gossip, email exchanges where they could impress others with their knowledge, developing powerpoint slides because they just didn't trust others to get them right. Of course, there is nothing wrong with these reasons, but the point is we need to be clear what our own sources of motivation are in order to help us decide what to delegate and what to keep control of.

Here are four techniques I have observed and experimented with over the years, all designed to help us become better at letting go:

Give up one visible element of control when you move into a new position. When Tony Blair became UK Prime Minister in 1997, he formally ceded control of the Bank of England to its Governor, a move that previous administrations had vehemently resisted. More prosaically, many people make symbolic changes when they move into a senior executive role, for example, giving up the corner office and moving into the middle of the open-plan area, or scrapping the executive dining room. Cynics will say this is just window-dressing and does not change the basic power structure of the organization, but I see such moves as a credible signal that the executive is looking for ways of reducing his or her control and is open to new ways of thinking.

Develop a signature practice that highlights your organization's commitment to letting go. Unlike the one-off change you make when moving into a new position, this is typically something you develop over time and formalize as a day-to-day practice that everyone participates in. I use the term "signature" here because the practice comes to represent a broader belief or value in the organization[6]. For example, the CEO of fund manager Bridgewater, Ray Dalio, makes a point of recording and archiving all internal meetings, to put substance behind his principles of transparency and accountability[7]. Nixon McInnes, a small UK-based consultancy, has values around empowerment, freedom-to-fail, and clear communication, and its signature practice is an open-salary policy, whereby individuals are personally responsible for proposing salary changes that are then reviewed by an elected group of colleagues. John Lewis, the UK retailer, gives the same annual bonus (as a percentage of salary) to all employees, as a way of reinforcing its partnership model.

Make a conscious plan to stop doing a few specific activities every week. The notion of writing a "stop doing" list to go with your "to do" list is well known, but very hard to implement. So I have developed a slight variant on this model, as follows. I ask managers to evaluate their planned activities over the next two weeks, to find out which ones they think are least important and most easily delegated (these are usually the same), and I ask them to identify five hours-worth of activities they can either drop or delegate. I then follow up with them afterwards to see how successful they were[8]. Some find it a useful forcing mechanism, and are immediately able to delegate tasks to their team-members or outsource them altogether; others really struggle to define meaningful chunks of work to get rid of or find themselves drawn back into meetings they had tried to get out of. Either way, it is quite an eye-opener for all of them in terms of how they can be most effective with their time.

Give your employees enough rope. Perhaps the hardest thing you can do as a boss is to let one of your team persevere with a project when your gut instinct tells you they are going in the wrong direction. Your controlling self (the elephant) wants to pull them back and give them the benefit of your experience, but your empowering self (the rider) knows that they need to figure it out for themselves. The simple advice here is *let them fail.* Of course you want to put a safety net in place, to make sure the fallout is minimized if the project fails, and you want to offer support and coaching along the way, but if you take the reins back mid-journey, the effect on the employee can be debilitating. Who is to say you are right anyway? I recall a conversation with Chris Bayliss, then head of Bank of New Zealand, who was pushing his branch managers to take much more responsibility. As he recalls,

"I went into this one branch and they'd got this children's party banner that said 'surprise, surprise', blu-tacked right across the line of tellers, completely contravening our usual policies. And I thought, what do I do, this is the test isn't it? I stood in the banking hall talking to the branch manager, I kept looking at this banner thinking okay how do I bring this up, I've got to coach and talk to him about it. And you know what, while we were stood there every bloody customer comes in and says to the tellers, what's the surprise? And you know what, the tellers had this brilliant script and I just stood there with my eyes open, thinking, well the customers don't seem to mind, the staff are on fire, and they're converting it into sales. So who's right and who's wrong?"

Letting go of power isn't rocket science – the basic tricks and techniques are obvious to everyone; it's just a matter of finding the ones that work for you. There is a caveat, of course, which is that letting go doesn't mean abrogating your responsibilities entirely. Good management involves keeping track of what your employees are up to, but without taking their accountability away. If I can boil this advice down to a single sentence, it reads as follows, with due apologies to Reinhold Neibhur, author of the serenity prayer: *"Grant me the courage to give power away, and the wisdom to know when to take it back."*

GIVING CREDIT TO OTHERS: WHY IS IT SO DIFFICULT?

The second basic principle of good management is to give credit to others – to recognize their achievements and to look for ways of enriching their work. However, this isn't an easy principle to live by, as it is human nature to take credit for your own achievements and indeed to believe that your own skills and capabilities are superior to those of the people around you.

Giving credit to others isn't quite the same as letting go, although obviously they are linked. Giving credit to others involves downplaying your *ego*; letting go involves downplaying your *involvement*. More often than not they are flip-sides of the same coin, but the underlying factors that shape them are different. Here is what we know from the psychology and behavioral economics research:

1. *The overconfidence bias.* Most people are overconfident in their own abilities, especially when those abilities are subjective. In one famous study, 93% of people claimed their driving skills were above the median level of the population. In another, 87% of MBA students at Stanford believed their grades placed them above the median in their class[9]. This is the so-called "better than average" effect. It has been observed in many settings and it is generally stronger among high-achieving people like managers.

2. *The illusion of skill.* Related to overconfidence is the tendency for experts to believe their professional skills are superior to others. When asked to forecast future events, for example, experts have been shown to score no better than the proverbial dart-throwing monkey, and the more those experts are in demand (e.g., TV pundits), the more overconfident their forecasts become[10].

3. *The optimism bias.* As well as being overconfident in their abilities, managers are optimistic about future events that are largely outside their control. For example, when entrepreneurs were asked about the prospects for their new business venture, 81% put the odds of success at 7 out of 10 or higher, but when asked the same question about a business like theirs, only 39% put the odds of success at 7 out of 10 or higher. Another study showed that 47% of entrepreneurs continued to invest in businesses that an expert panel had rated as hopeless and on average they doubled their losses before subsequently giving up[11].

4. *Power drives dominant behavior.* There is an enormous body of research looking at the many ways people placed in positions of power change their behavior towards others. Most readers will have heard of the famous Stanford prison studies by Philip Zimbardo, in which the students acting as "guards"

quickly became abusive towards their fellow students who were designated as "prisoners." A more recent example, from psychologist Dan Ariely, is the social experiment in which a plate of cookies is left on the table around which three subjects work. One subject is given a boss-like role, the other two are subordinates. Sure enough, after each person has eaten one cookie, it is the boss who takes the initiative to eat the fourth cookie. Power, in other words, encourages bosses to behave in various domineering ways over their underlings, and those underlings are usually quick to fall in line.

If you take these four points together, you end up with a fairly predictable set of consequences. The manager is convinced of his or her own superior skills and judgment and takes credit for the achievements of the team. The team then reinforce his or her self-image, because the manager is in a position of power over them. Taken in aggregate, this pattern of behavior has been observed in many different contexts. For example, studies have shown how overconfident and egotistical CEOs make more risky and expensive acquisitions, and fail to heed the warning signs when things go wrong[12]. My colleague, Nigel Nicholson, did a study of UK corporate leaders a few years back and found them to be "single minded, thick skinned, dominating individuals.[13]"

GIVING CREDIT TO OTHERS: SOME ADVICE ON DOING IT BETTER

So how can *you* become more effective at giving credit to others and downplaying your own achievements? A useful analogy is to the world of share trading. Because we are loss-averse, our instinct is to harvest our winnings and to retain poorly performing investments in the hope that they will rebound. However, a much better strategy is to do the exact opposite – *to cut your losses and ride your winners*. Even though professional traders know this, they still need the message to be reinforced on a continuous basis, because it goes so sharply against their instincts.

I propose a similar mantra for you as a manager: *own your failures, share your successes.* Your natural predisposition is to do the opposite, so as a rule of thumb, as a guide to behavior when you are uncertain how to proceed, sharing your successes is almost always the right way forward. For example, Vineet Nayar, former CEO of HCL Technologies, has spoken about "destroying the office of the CEO" as a way of spreading accountability across the company and reducing the amount of credit he receives for the company's successes.

As with letting go, there are some specific techniques that you can employ to make this a bit more practical for yourself, whatever position you sit in within your organization.

Work yourself out of a job. Each level of management adds value to the one below. Well, that is the intention. In reality, there are often overlapping roles between layers in a hierarchy, leading to disagreement and frustration. So one useful way of approaching an executive job is to imagine that the role won't exist in, say, two years' time, and your job is to train everyone up so that they make you redundant. I have personal experience of doing this when I was given a three-year position as a Deputy Dean at London Business School, and it was a really useful way of approaching the job. It encouraged me to hire and promote the best people, it forced me to question why I did certain things at all, and it inspired me to delegate many of my tasks to the people working for me.

Now I realize this approach is risky. If your enlightened approach to management is not shared by *your* boss, it is possible that the goal of "working yourself out of a job" may actually end up with you having no job. In my experience, however, this discipline of pushing as much work down as possible actually had the effect of changing the nature of the work I did as a manager – it forced me to spend more time on mentoring and supporting activities and it resulted in better performance all round.

In a related way, I have sometimes observed that interim managers are often more effective than permanent ones. This is in large part because they see their job as enabling others, rather than making themselves indispensable. They typically see their job as "making the trains run on time" rather than imposing a grand new strategy on the organization. Often this approach inspires those around them to take more responsibility and work more effectively.

Package work– even routine work – into projects. As discussed in Chapter 2, when I ask managers about a piece of work they did where they felt fully engaged and motivated, they talk about it being challenging, worthwhile, and free from interference. Importantly, they almost always find themselves recalling a discrete project. This isn't surprising, but it is interesting, because it suggests that one way of giving more credit and responsibility to others is to structure work into a series of projects. The essence of a project is simply: (a) a clear objective, (b) a deadline by which the objective needs to be reached, and (c) a clear sense of who is doing the work and who is responsible. It doesn't take a great deal of imagination to see how much of the day-to-day work we do could be repackaged in such a way. Indeed, many organizations already play these games. For example, fundraising is a never-ending activity in a university, but to make it more motivating for fundraisers and donors alike, it gets packaged around a series of campaigns. Once one campaign is over, the fundraising team celebrate and start all over again. It is worth considering whether you can do something similar in your organization, by chunking routine work into a series of projects.

A related approach is to be more creative at carving out semi-autonomous pieces of work within a larger project. You may be responsible for the entire project, but if your employee can own one piece of it, and attach his or her name to it, then your needs and that of the employee will both be met. In a very different setting, this was the approach adopted by Antoni Gaudi when he put together the blueprint for the Sagrada Familia church in Barcelona. Realizing that it would not be finished until well after his death, Gaudi encouraged other architects to create their own designs within his own master plan, to ensure that they felt some ownership for the work.

Nurture your critics and own up to your mistakes. Finally, there are aspects of your personal management style that are closely linked to your capacity to give credit to others. One is a capacity to take personal responsibility for problems that emerge on your watch, whether or not they were of your own making. Writing this book immediately after the London Olympics, I recall the grovelling apologies made by Nick Buckles, CEO of G4S, the huge contracting company that failed to hire enough security people before the Olympics started. Clearly, the mistakes were made several levels below Buckles, but he took it on the chin and accepted that he, personally, had let the British people down. Unfortunately, the ability to say "sorry, I was wrong" is one that the vast majority of managers struggle with. A survey by the Belgium-based Krauthammer Observatory asked employees whether their managers would spontaneously take responsibility when mistakes were made: 48% said yes. This is a long way behind the 92% of respondents who said they wished their managers would act in this way.

So how can you become better at taking ownership of your failures? One prerequisite is unfiltered feedback, that is, advice and evidence that tells you when things have not gone well. Some organizations push the principle of straight-talking, whether boss to subordinate, subordinate to boss, or peer to peer. At Intel this principle is called *Constructive Confrontation*; at McKinsey it is called the *Obligation to Dissent*; at Bridgewater Associates it is called *Radical Transparency*. Ray Dalio, the Bridgewater CEO, observes, "I believe that the biggest problem that humanity faces is an *ego* sensitivity to finding out whether one is right or wrong and identifying what one's strengths and weaknesses are.[14]" So he has deliberately pushed an organizational model that encourages brutally honest feedback.

If you don't work for a company that takes feedback seriously, you have to nurture your own critics: sometimes this is an executive coach; sometimes it is personal friends with no immediate stake in your success; sometimes it is an anonymized 360 review that gives your subordinates a licence to say what they really think. In economist Tim Harford's terms, these people represent a *validation squad* who can help you overcome your enormous capacity for self-delusion[15].

SELF-CONTROL: WHY IS IT SO DIFFICULT?

The third principle of good management is self-control – the ability to regulate your own emotions and instincts. As we have seen, good management is often about overcoming your natural instincts, but not always. There are times when an emotional response is more powerful than a rational one and there are some situations where a "gut" decision is better than the one reached through careful analysis. So if the two previous principles were essentially about downplaying your instincts, this one is about learning how to strike a balance – about knowing yourself so well that you can switch back and forth between the two different modes of operating: emotional versus rational behavior or intuitive versus analytical decision-making.

Let's be clear: self-control as I am describing it here is really hard to achieve. In many situations, we don't have time to metaphorically stand back and decide how we will respond. Moreover, if we behave in a way that doesn't look natural to those around us, we come across as devious and lacking in authenticity. So the message is *not* to abandon your natural style of working. Rather, it is to be sufficiently knowledgeable about the benefits and limitations of your natural style that you can catch yourself before you make a blunder. Here is a simple personal example: my natural style in a meeting is to be logical and calm, and to be agreeable with those around me. These are often very helpful traits, but occasionally, if a decision is contentious, I run the risk of looking ineffectual. So I have learnt to push back every now and then, and respond with more emotion.

What does research tell us about self-control? A great deal, it turns out. Here are some highlights:

1. *Subconscious cues affect how we behave.* Without us knowing it, we are influenced through words, images, and physical stimuli that "prime" us to behave in a certain way. For example, a study of voting behavior in Arizona showed that propositions to increase school funding received more support when the polling station was in a school than when it was in another type of location. A study of students in the UK showed that a photo of a pair of eyes placed above the "honesty box" (into which the students put a small sum of money every time they made a cup of coffee) increased the level of payments significantly[16]. Studies have even sought to understand the effect of money as a priming device, for example, by placing a pile of monopoly money on a table or asking subjects to create a money-related phrase out of a list of words. Scarily, subjects primed to think of money subsequently became more independent-minded, more selfish, and less willing to help others[17]. The point, in a nutshell, is that we are in less control of our behavior than we think we are.

2. *Our conscious mind is easily exhausted.* Because many of the demands we face as managers require conscious effort, we often end up mentally exhausted, a state of mind referred to as *ego depletion*, and we end up lapsing back into a default mode of operating that relies more on System 1 than System 2, where the elephant, not the rider, is in charge. Self-control, in other words, is a limited resource. For example, a study of eight parole judges in Israel sought to understand whether extraneous factors influenced their decision-making. They would spend the entire day reviewing parole applications. The default was denial, with only 35% of requests approved. However, the study showed that the proportion of approvals spiked after each meal, rising to as much as 65% being

approved, then it dropped steadily until the next meal came along. The researchers concluded that tired and hungry judges tend to fall back on the easier default position of denying requests for parole[18].

The practical lesson for all of us is clear: if we want to make difficult decisions – ones that go against priming and experience – we should do it when we are well rested and well fed. More broadly, it is useful to know what our general state of mind is before performing our various managerial duties. Daniel Kahneman has shown that when in a state of "cognitive ease" we are more creative and intuitive, and less careful, whereas in a state of "cognitive stress" we tend to be more analytical and suspicious.

3. *Expert intuition is a dangerous master.* Many readers will be familiar with Malcolm Gladwell's best-seller, *Blink*, which showed how experts often make snap judgments without knowing quite how. Research evidence in this field paints a complex and sometimes worrying picture. Sometimes the intuitive judgment of the expert proves accurate, but at other times a more analytical approach wins out. For example, a famous book by Paul Meehl showed how statistical predictions (based on hard data) were superior to clinical predictions (based on expert judgment) in the fields of psychology and medicine[19], while Orley Ashenfelter showed that the future value of wine could be predicted more accurately by measures of the weather when the grapes were grown than by the estimates of the wine experts[20].

We should be cautious, in other words, when relying on our intuitive expertise. Unfortunately, most executives don't want to heed this advice: research has shown that being in a position of power makes people more, not less, likely to simply follow their gut instinct[21].

Put the findings from these studies together and again the net effect is predictable. Even as respected and thoughtful executives, we frequently become cognitively lazy: we go with the flow, in terms of what our System 1 thought processes steer us towards; we allow our behavior to be primed by the situation in which we find ourselves; and we make snap decisions, convinced that expertise dominates analysis. Sometimes this approach goes horribly wrong: recall, for example, Fred Goodwin's 2007 decision that RBS should buy ABN AMRO, based essentially on his gut feeling that the opportunity was comparable to the company's acquisition of NatWest bank a decade earlier. However, intuitive decision-making can also go spectacularly right, so the point here is not that you should always trust your rational mind, rather that you should become more conscious of the balance between the two sides.

SELF-CONTROL: SOME ADVICE ON DOING IT BETTER

So how can we increase our capacity for self-control? This is one of the most fundamental questions in psychology, and there are several fields of thinking from Cognitive Behavioral Therapy to Psychotherapy that seek to answer it. I will focus here on self-control in the business world, but for interested readers there are applications to many aspects of life[22].

> *Become more attentive to your own shortcomings.* We are prone to cognitive laziness. We fall back on learned behaviors and we let our habits take over. To break out of this cycle, we need to develop little tricks and stimuli to make us more attentive, more aware of our shortcomings.
>
> I find the following metaphor useful. Karl Weick is a leading social psychologist based at the University of Michigan and during the 1990s he studied what he called "high-reliability organizations" such as aircraft carriers and nuclear power stations, where the tolerance for error was close to zero[23]. We all know that people get into behavioral routines at work, where they allow their subconscious mind to take over. Weick discovered that these high-reliability organizations had created

mechanisms and norms of behavior that encouraged employees to transcend these routines. There was a "refusal to simplify" complex situations, a preoccupation with potential failure, and a fluid approach to organizational structure, with people apparently duplicating effort and moving between roles. These mechanisms helped to create "mindfulness" across the organization. In other words, they were designed to prevent employees from lapsing into mindless routines.

Many organizations in the extraction and manufacturing sector nowadays take these ideas about high reliability very seriously. I work with a large mining company and its approach to safety borders on the obsessive. The first 10 minutes of every meeting are devoted to safety issues, with attendees talking about recent safety incidents or offering tips to their colleagues. Conference calls with investors start with an update on safety, before the financial information is presented. This constant repetition is their way of keeping safety in the conscious part of the mind. By reminding themselves that safety matters, even when it doesn't, the employees of this company stay attentive and vigilant.

So how can you apply this logic to your *own* behavior? Recall the example of the pair of eyes placed above the coffee pot in the student residence. While operating at a subconscious level, this is the equivalent of the mining company's daily safety share – a constant reminder that we want to behave in an honest and ethical way. Dan Ariely, a leading figure in the world of behavioral economics, has done many experiments in this area, for example, asking people to sign their tax return *before* filling it in, to encourage them to disclose all their taxable earnings. His conclusion is simple but profound: "While ethics lectures have little to no effect, reminders of morality, right at the point where people are making a decision, appear to have an outsize effect on behavior.[24]"

The implications for you as a manager are straightforward: you can create simple stimuli, from a note on your diary, to a poster on your wall, to a conversation with a coach or mentor, prior to important meetings or conversations. These stimuli serve to remind you what is important and reduce your tendency to lapse back into routine or subconscious behaviors.

Be explicit about why your intuition goes against the empirical data. As we saw above, experts and powerful people have an enormous amount of belief in their own wisdom. Fred Goodwin, the former CEO of Royal Bank of Scotland, was reported to have a "5-second rule" for making decisions. Jack Welch, former CEO of GE, was also a famous believer in the power of experience-based decision-making – as his biography, *Straight from the Gut,* made clear. However, the other side of the argument is also compelling. Here is Jeff Bezos, current CEO of Amazon.com: "For every leader in the company, not just for me, there are decisions that can be made by analysis. These are the best kinds of decisions!" Also, "The most junior person in the company can win an argument with the most senior person with a fact-based decision."

So which is it? Should you follow your gut or should you let the empirical analysis guide you? Well the answer, as always, is that it depends, but to make this facile statement a bit more useful, I propose another metaphor, which I call *Managing by GPS* (or Managing by SatNav for UK readers). Most drivers today have access to GPS technology, which provides a recommended route based on the available information. So when faced with a proposed route in a town you know well, do you follow it carefully? Or do you take a different route, because you believe you know better? I have been experimenting with myself here and I have quickly come to two conclusions: (1) if I always follow the GPS route, I occasionally get into trouble; (2) if I choose my own route, I occasionally come out ahead, but usually find myself lost or following an inferior route. These insights have led me to the following strategy: whenever I believe I know a better route than the one the GPS is suggesting, I ask myself, on what basis? If I know there has been an accident, or bad traffic, things the GPS cannot possibly be factoring in, then I go with my choice. However, if I cannot make a rational case to myself, then I (reluctantly) follow the GPS advice.

Hopefully the lesson from this metaphor is clear: many of your decisions as a manager are based on the equivalent of a GPS route – a report or a proposal that provides the best possible advice on the basis of the readily available data. It is your prerogative to overturn the advice you receive, but before doing so you should justify – to yourself – the basis for your judgment. Unless you can find an explanation, based on your personal experience and breadth of knowledge, you are better advised to stick to the proposed course of action.

The world of fund management provides a nice example of this. As a fund manager, it is tempting to follow your gut, perhaps because you have been successful with a particular strategy before, perhaps because you are being swayed by those around you. However, there is mounting evidence that persistent success in fund management comes from a highly rational approach, built around an individual's area of deep expertise and a careful monitoring of hit-rates (how many picks ended up making money?) and win–loss ratios (did the winners offset the losers?). As Simon Savage of MAN Group (a UK investment company) observes, "It is possible to detect and progressively control inherent biases. This can be facilitated through an objective feedback process, which helps to nurture investment talent and improve the quality of decision making over time.[25]" In other words, even a highly subjective activity such as investing can benefit from a data-driven approach, as a way of overcoming our inherent biases.

OVERCOMING OUR NATURAL INSTINCTS

The world of business is filled with managers like yourself who are seeking to become more effective in their work. However, the evidence suggests the gap between what we want to achieve and what we are able to achieve is as big as ever. I spend a lot of time working with companies on these issues and one of the interventions I often get involved in is small-scale experiments, such as the If insurance one at the beginning of this chapter. Very often, the experiment is a success, but the real insight ends being: So why don't we just do this stuff anyway?

Lack of time and resources is only part of the story. I think the underlying problem is that so many aspects of good management involve going against our natural instincts. We have to work very hard to overcome our need for control and our bias for self-aggrandizement. We also have to be very self-aware to realize when our behavioral flaws are getting in the way. There are no simple solutions here, but hopefully this chapter has offered some useful tips and tricks to help you be more aware of your own shortcomings and more thoughtful about ways of overcoming them.

Of course, even the most thoughtful and deliberate managers can still see their efforts come to nothing, if they cannot rely on the rest of the organization to support them. We would like to believe our organizations were designed to help us. Unfortunately, that is only partially true. Even the best-functioning organizations have flaws and pathologies that often get in our way. So good management isn't just about understanding our own limitations, it is also about understanding our organization's limitations and what we can do to transcend them. That is the subject of the next chapter.

— 6 —

EXPERIMENTATION: FUNCTIONING IN A BROKEN SYSTEM

Have you ever tried anything a bit risky in your company: an idea that no-one had pushed before or a project that required people across the company to act in new ways? If you have, you probably felt you succeeded *despite the system* rather than because of it. Rather than help you in your endeavor, the people and processes surrounding you conspired to hold you back, and it was only through tenacity and resolve that you were able to prevail.

I have quite a lot of personal experience of how this happens and I have observed dozens of similar cases through my research. It is easy to conclude that the "system" in large organizations is broken. However, this is only half true. Large organizations do indeed suffer from acute limitations and bizarre pathologies, but they also have enormous strengths that we should not lose sight of. Being an effective manager requires a deep understanding of the limitations *and* strengths of the organization in which you are working.

Here is a cautionary tale from my own experience. I once agreed to do a Webinar for a big organization. I have done half-a-dozen Webinars before, typically for small companies trying to get people to pay for online content. In these cases, the process looks like this: they email me, I agree to do it, we arrange a date 2–3 months out, we do a quick technology check the week before, and then the event happens. It is all very easy, lecturing to an unseen audience in my own office. Frankly, I sometimes wonder how many people are actually listening. But that is a separate issue.

The process with this particular organization was rather different. The person I was talking to suggested a multispeaker event six months out. The other speakers and I all said yes. He then consulted with his board, who decided it was all a bit rushed, and couldn't be marketed properly, so we ended up delaying by a further six months. We all agreed.

A couple of months later I received the draft contract, 10 pages of detailed legalese, including clauses restricting my use of the presentation materials with other audiences, and requiring me to acknowledge them in all subsequent use of the materials. At which point it finally dawned on me what was going on – the Webinar was being treated like a book, one of those bulky paper things we used to take on holiday with us before the Kindle was invented. Once I had taken out the clauses that restricted my use of my own materials, the final version was then sent to me in hardcopy, by courier – one of those companies that was set up to distribute paper around the world before the Internet was invented.

The company had, in other words, taken its century-old process for selection and negotiating rights and applied it with little adjustment to these new digital and virtual offerings. My realization that this is what happened also explained the mystery around the six-month delay. Every publisher knows that books either get published in spring or fall; that is the way the publishing calendar works. So once our Webinar missed the spring window, it obviously had to be bumped to an autumn date.

I know I am being a bit harsh on the organization here. The people who work there are smart and knowledgeable and they understand these new technologies as well as I do. But they are being held hostage by their archaic management processes, processes that they themselves curse but are incapable of getting around. The net result, in this particular case, was a Webinar that cost a great deal to put on (in management time and legal fees) and with significant delays. When the event finally happened it went fine, but the size of the audience and the quality of the product were no better or worse than the low-cost, no-frills Webinars I had done before.

UNDERSTANDING BUREAUCRACY – AND RISING ABOVE IT

This experience reinforced for me just how inert and inflexible management processes are in most large organizations. A company can change its strategy, replace all its senior managers, outsource half its activities, and even get people thinking differently, but its core management processes – the way it allocates resources, evaluates people, negotiates contracts – will still be running under their own steam, just as they did decades earlier.

Management processes are the embodiment of an organization principle known as bureaucracy. We all know the word, and we often use it as a shorthand for everything that is bad about large organizations. Strangely, though, the original meaning of bureaucracy was entirely positive. German sociologist Max Weber brought the term into regular usage. He said organizations could coordinate activity in one of three ways: by using the traditional beliefs and norms of what had always been done ("traditional" domination); by relying on the personality of their leader ("charismatic" domination); or by developing a system of rules and procedures that transcended the idiosyncrasies of a particular person or situation ("legal" domination). This third model, which came to be known as bureaucracy, dominated the business world during the twentieth century, and was indeed very effective as a means of generating efficiency and creating outputs with consistent quality.

However, bureaucratic systems also have their limitations. They create a high level of alienation and disengagement among employees. They allow people to exercise their power in ways that subvert the organization's broader goals. They also breed management processes that take on a life of their own and never die out. At their worst, bureaucratic organizations are made up of unhappy employees, Machiavellian managers, and internally focused processes where no-one can see the forest for the trees.

What can we do to overcome these deep pathologies? One way forward is to attempt to make organizations less bureaucratic. If you have ever picked up a book by Tom Peters, Rosabeth Moss Kanter, or Gary Hamel, you will have seen plenty of advice on how to de-bureaucratize the business world, such as pushing greater front-line accountability, eliminating mid-management roles, encouraging spin-offs, and so on. These are all sensible suggestions but they don't "solve" the problems of bureaucracy, they simply keep them under control.

The other way forward, and my focus here, is for individuals to find more effective ways of working within this "broken" system. In other words, as a manager, you learn to accept that the system has certain limits, and you make sufficient changes within your sphere of influence to get things done. For example, in one research project I was involved in, the evidence showed clearly that the more complex the system, the more important it was for individuals to be multitasking, proactive types who were able to "rise above the nonsense" to make things happen.

So if the previous two chapters were about understanding and remedying our insensitivity to our employees, and our own personal biases, this chapter is about recognizing the limitations and pathologies of the organization that surrounds us – and finding ways of coping. As suggested in Figure 6.1, bureaucracy has three primary pathologies.

First, it results in *alienation* – a feeling of disillusionment or detachment on the part of the individual worker, when he is separated from the product of his labour. This was Karl Marx's insight, and of course it led him down a path towards class warfare and communism that proved to be a dead end[1]. However, his original insight was spot on, and the need to find ways of helping workers to become more involved in their work and in the fruits of their efforts is as great as it has ever been.

Figure 6.1   The Problems with Bureaucracy and How to Cope

PROBLEMS WITH BUREAUCRACY	COPING STRATEGIES
ALIENATION Individuals are separated from the outputs of their work, which breeds disillusionment and detachment	**MAKE WORK MORE ENGAGING** Look for creative ways of helping employees to gain intrinsic motivation from their work (see Chapters 4 and 5)
POLITICAL GAME-PLAYING Individuals follow their personal agendas with little regard for their impact on the organization as a whole	**TAKE PERSONAL INITIATIVE** Use the principles of *real politik* to generate support, build allies and neutralize the concerns of your critics
INERT PROCEDURES The processes and rules for getting work done take on a life of their own, and are almost impossible to kill	**CHALLENGE THE RULES** Put in place small-scale experiments to show how existing procedures can be removed or replaced with better ones

Second, bureaucracy gives rise to political *game-playing*. The definitive insight here came from the French sociologist, Michel Crozier, who observed that so much of what happens in bureaucracies is decided in advance, that the only way people are able to gain some control over their working lives is to exploit "zones of uncertainty" where the outcomes are not already known[2]. Thus, interactions in large organizations become a series of games and power struggles, in which people pursue their personal agendas, with little or no regard for their effect on the organization as a whole.

I doubt I need to convince you that big organizations are hotbeds of political maneuvring and game-playing. Some managers are simply self-interested, only contributing to a cause when it suits their immediate needs to do so. Others are schemers, taking delight in sabotaging the plans of others as a way of furthering their own agenda. Of course, not all managers act in these ways, but if even a minority do, it means everyone else has to adapt their behavior accordingly.

Third, bureaucracy *allows inert procedures* to emerge. As we saw with my Webinar story above, these processes take on a life of their own and are almost impossible to kill. They support the primary value-adding activities of the firm, but they are often two or three steps removed from the marketplace, so feedback from customers gets filtered out and lost. They have their own managers, who have strong vested interests in keeping their jobs. These processes are dependent on each other, creating a tightly woven matrix of activities that cannot easily be pulled apart. The budgeting process is perhaps the definitive example, a process that according to one book is "time-consuming, adds little value, and prevents managers responding quickly to changes in the business environment.[3]"

Most of the previous two chapters were about finding antidotes to alienation, for example, by getting inside the mind of our employees and looking for creative ways of making their work more fulfilling. So I won't give this issue any further consideration in this chapter. Instead, I will focus on the second and third pathologies. We can overcome political game-playing through personal initiative – by rising above the petty games of our colleagues and by coming up with creative ways of making a difference. We can also overcome our inert procedures by seeking out creative ways of challenging them or renewing them.

Experimentation as a guiding metaphor. The theme that is pursued throughout this chapter is experimentation – the notion that we can make changes through low-risk, carefully planned changes in how work gets done. When I lecture on management, I often use examples of innovative organizational models put in place by visionary CEOs, such as Vineet Nayar at HCL Technologies, AG Lafley at Procter & Gamble, or Lars Kolind at a Danish hearing aid company, Oticon. However, for mid-level managers, these stories are more likely to be a source of frustration than inspiration, because *their* CEO and executive team are not taking such bold steps.

The truth is, though, that cases of successful, top-down transformation are rare, and even when they occur they typically involve a lot of small-scale, under-the-radar experiments that collectively make the overall transformation possible.

So my advice to mid-level managers is always the same. You cannot change the entire system. You also cannot afford to ignore the rules altogether, because you will be out of a job before you know it. So the way forward is management experimentation – a conscious and structured process for putting in place new ways of working. I will get into a detailed discussion of the hallmarks of a good experiment later in the chapter, but at a minimum it requires a clear hypothesis (for example, if we give employees 4 hours a week "dabble-time" innovation will increase); it is limited in its scope and duration to keep the level of risk under control; and it takes place in a real-world setting, to ensure the findings are meaningful. The If insurance example in the previous chapter was a classic experiment, as it represented an explicit test of the hypothesis that greater coaching of employees by a front-line supervisor would increase their sales competence.

Let's take a look at the different ways experimentation can help you to overcome the political game-playing and inert procedures in your organization.

TAKE PERSONAL INITIATIVE – TO OVERCOME POLITICAL GAME-PLAYING

When something isn't working very well, you can take the path of least resistance and just put up with it or you can follow the path less travelled and try to improve it. This was the crossroads that Jordan Cohen, Director of Organizational Effectiveness at Pfizer, was standing at in 2005. He realized people were wasting a lot of time on low-value, run-of-the-mill work, like building spreadsheets, booking travel, and doing background research. Given the enormous cost pressure the company was under at the time, this seemed like an obvious area where greater efficiency was possible. "I noticed one of my team, Paul, an MIT graduate, spending time after hours doing tasks that were not just below his pay-grade but not core to his role either," he recalls. "I knew there had to be a way to unburden him from this low-value work.[4]"

Pfizer wasn't an organization that encouraged bold moves. It was a leader in a highly profitable and highly regulated industry, and it exercised due caution at every turn.

Seeking to turn his observations about Paul into something tangible, he drew inspiration from Tom Friedman's *The World is Flat*, which opened up his eyes to the possibility of taking advantage of the global marketplace for services. He came to the realization that outsourcing could be done at a microlevel, around individual tasks. The pitch to his colleagues was: "I think I can help by delivering that to your inbox within 24 hours so you don't have to do it . . . it may cost a little bit of money but it will be just as good as if you did it" (note that he did not say, "I can outsource this for you" – he quickly learned that the term outsourcing had negative connotations). This resonated strongly across the company, and it gave him the impetus to turn his idea into an experiment.

Jordan first collected some data, and he was able to show that colleagues were spending 20–40% of their time on noncore work. He immersed himself in the practice of outsourcing, developing detailed knowledge of the types of services readily available, how to select and manage vendors, and how to ensure a high-quality service. By working evenings and weekends, Jordan was able to design a prototype program within just a few months – a service that colleagues could access at the click of a button, to secure one-stop support for such things as business research, data analysis, and creating documents.

Having a working prototype allowed Jordan's colleagues to start using the service and for him to learn how to make it work properly. As he recalls, "When I first started this, I didn't know what I was doing. By the time I finished, I was an expert. We weren't just looking at the output on a monthly or weekly basis, we were looking at it every night, and we were putting fixes in place immediately." Plenty of mistakes were made – "I personally bought a lot of drinks for people, I apologized, that's what you do" – but within one year the service was operating in pilot form.

Moving from the pilot to a fully fledged operation took another year. Getting the name right was a challenge. *Virtual assistance* was Cohen's first proposal, but it sent the wrong message to the firm's secretaries who worried they were being replaced. *Office of the Future* became the working title, which gave way eventually to *PfizerWorks*. Cohen also had to get buy-in at every level, even meeting with the CEO to get the final endorsement to proceed.

Jordan didn't face any outright hostility in pursuing this initiative. In fact, no-one ever told him it was a bad idea, but there was a real risk of death by a thousand cuts. Some people were sceptical. Others were disinterested. Most had better things to do than help him. Faced with this mass indifference, he could easily have given up, but instead he chose to rise above it, and get PfizerWorks off the ground. So what were the tactics he adopted? What advice does he have for others who would like to transcend the narrow personal agendas of their colleagues?

Stay under the radar for as long as possible. A new idea can often look completely crazy when it is first proposed, and it will have plenty of bugs or ill-thought-out elements that make it an easy target for critics. So the first point is simply to keep a low profile in the early stages and to resolve the initial problems that you encounter. As Cohen explained, "You try to keep it under the radar for a long time. All the while, you are learning, gaining confidence, you are spending money, and starting to resource it." Cohen was in a role – senior director of organizational effectiveness – where he had some licence for dabbling in new projects, but even so he realised the need for caution in straying too far into other people's territories. "At some point," though, "you have no choice to get above the radar, but you have to be very deliberate about that."

Make a clear link to the agenda of those at the top. One of the central features of bureaucracy is that everyone has a personal agenda, a set of things they are trying to achieve within their own area of discretion. So in designing an experiment, you need to show how it aligns with the interests of those who have some influence over its long-term success. For Cohen, the first port of call was his direct boss. He wrote a note about the PfizerWorks concept into his personal objectives, "So that if I was successful, he would get credit for it." But more importantly, Cohen also saw an opportunity to link his idea to a big initiative the CEO of Pfizer was pushing, called *Adapting to Scale*: "This was an effort to actually look at the way we're doing things, to see if we were using the scale that Pfizer has, in purchasing power, knowledge sharing, and so on. By positioning PfizerWorks as an Adapting to Scale initiative, I was able to get the air cover I needed to move forward."

Provide hard evidence – using traditional metrics. Once the initial technical issues with PfizerWorks had been overcome, Cohen faced the broader challenge of showing how the company as a whole would benefit from it. There were plenty of fence-sitters and sceptics in those first few years, who saw it as an interesting plaything, not as a serious business activity. Cohen realized he needed to run Pfizer using metrics everyone would understand. "You have to put it in the language of business," he observes, "because when decision-making happens, people need an apples-to-apples comparison. So I started calculating how much time people were spending doing the tasks they were subcontracting to our team of virtual assistants. This allowed me to create impact metrics – so I could report, on a monthly basis, how many hours and how many dollars had been saved, and what the level of service was like." Armed with these metrics, Cohen was able to give an order-of-magnitude assessment of the value of PfizerWorks, and this was enough to get the project implemented on an ongoing basis.

Find the right partners to take it forward. Machiavelli wrote of the lukewarm supporters and committed enemies that surround every new idea. Of course, an experimental approach is deliberately designed to keep the critics at bay, because its default status is to stop, rather than to continue. But sooner or later, a worthwhile initiative needs to become a serious change project and at this point you need partners and supporters.

Cohen has some very clear advice here. As well as getting his boss on board early, he also built a web of partners inside and outside Pfizer. Internally, he worked with a core group of "friendlies" – people who he had an existing relationship with, who would give him good feedback. Externally, he found some suppliers who would partner with him at minimal cost. However, once the project started to gather some steam, he realized there were some important capabilities he didn't have. For example, as a headquarters-based manager, his knowledge of the field force was limited. So rather than spending a lot of time building field credibility, he opted to bring in a team member who really understood the field.

In sum, Jordan Cohen made PfizerWorks a success through the corporate equivalent of *real politik* – a strategy built around understanding and responding to the personal interests of those around him. The tactics he pursued were all about avoiding or defusing criticism, and gaining support among those who could help him to make PfizerWorks a success. In an ideal world, where organizations worked without flaws, he could have focused purely on getting the technical aspects of the project right, but by recognizing the inherent limitations of a huge company like Pfizer, and responding appropriately, he was able to make the project a success.

CHALLENGE THE RULES – TO OVERCOME INERT PROCEDURES

Jordan Cohen's tale is one of patience and tenacity, of accepting the constraints of the system and working within and across them to get things done. All credit to him – many people would have simply given up somewhere along the way.

However, there is another way forward when faced with a wall of resistance to your well-intentioned initiatives: namely, to set about tearing the wall down, brick by brick if necessary. Of course, I am not going to recommend you pursue a sophisticated form of career suicide. Deliberately breaking the rules can work, but it can be very dangerous as well[5]. I recommend a more prudent approach. The starting point is to be very clear on your own degrees of freedom – your level of authority and the tolerance for change of those to whom you are accountable.

So here is an important question: Are you the boss? And when I say boss, I mean is there an area of business that you are fully accountable for? This could be an entire corporation or more likely a single business unit, function, or department. If you are, then you have the opportunity to "just do it." Of course, there is still an issue of how you manage up, to keep those above you informed and on-board, but that shouldn't stop you from doing what needs to be done. Here are two examples of top-down approaches.

Decentralization at Bank of New Zealand[6]. Chris Bayliss took over as head of Bank of New Zealand's retail operations in 2006 (he subsequently left the bank in 2012). At that point, the trend was towards centralization, with strong back-office functions and standardized systems to drive greater efficiency. Bayliss felt this was taking banking in the wrong direction. There are basically two ways you can run a retail network for a bank: one is you assume head office knows best and the branch manager's job is to implement company policy; the other is you assume the people running the branches probably know best. Bayliss was clear which model he preferred: "I strongly believe that front-line staff know much better than me how to run their local businesses. I wanted them to feel – and act – like it was their own business."

This view led Bayliss to formulate a couple of initial experiments, one allowing branch managers to set their own opening hours, the other giving them control over their marketing budgets. "Within six months, nearly 95% of our stores had altered their hours in some way, to better serve their local customers. For example, in one Auckland suburb, we became the first bank to open on a Sunday morning, allowing us to service the thousands of customers who flooded the local farmers' market." While these experiments were, naturally enough, popular with branch managers, they led to some surprising new insights. Many branch managers, for example, didn't have the skills or courage to be effective in this new empowered workplace. Bayliss also had to work hard to overcome objections from some corporate functions. HR was concerned that changing hours would raise objections from the employee union, so store managers had to get agreement from all employees. Marketing also thought that the hand-lettered signs being used to advertise store hours looked tacky, so they developed a software template that allowed store managers to print out a simple sign with store hours. The results of these changes had a rapid impact, with 10% growth in sales after the first year and employee engagement ratings at around 85%.

How did he get support for these changes? The challenge was one of managing "sideways:" persuading the corporate HR team, the technology people, the risk function, and the corporate branding team that these changes had very little downside and a lot of upside. So at the end of the day it was about educating them: "I'm a great believer in storytelling and what we did is we were very effective at promoting best practice and telling the stories of the successes."

Building a trust-based culture in Microsoft. Ross Smith – whom we met briefly in Chapter 4 – became director of the Windows Security Test Team in 2006, in charge of 85 people doing high-intensity, high-value, if somewhat unsexy work. He met with each one individually and recalls being staggered at the potential and capability of the team[7]. "I wondered if we could bring that potential to bear inside Microsoft's walls. To create an environment where the team could have more freedom with the 'how' rather than be relentlessly preoccupied with the 'what.'" Without a specific end-goal in mind, Smith started a series of internal management experiments all designed to harness the productivity and creativity of his team. He started with a bottom-up investigation of the drivers of trust, with 40% of the team actively participating through a wiki-based discussion forum. A weekly free-pizza meeting, starting in

2007, allowed people to discuss their ideas in a more personal setting. Some web-based tools for sharing information about project status, submitting calls for help, and promoting new ideas were introduced. They gave the programme a name – 42Projects (from the *Hitch Hiker's Guide to the Galaxy*) – to reflect their quirky worldview.

It's not easy to put your finger on exactly what Ross Smith's experiment was, but that's partly the point. He knew the traditional hierarchical model of management wasn't going to work for him, or his team. But trust and creativity aren't things you can mandate, so instead he threw the responsibility for defining them back to the team – he gave them the tools and the space to experiment and he waited to see what would emerge. Not surprisingly, the team responded enthusiastically. Mark McDonald, Microsoft's first employee, a friend of Bill Gates in high school and a key member of the team, observed, "42Projects tries to recapture the feeling and passion you have at a small startup or at the beginning of an industry by breaking down the stratification of a large organization." Mark Hanson, another team member, concurs: "We're giving people the latitude to go off and do their own thing. We trust them to do their regular jobs and to experiment, innovate, and have fun. We're developing a level of trust where there's no required accountability that you need to log your time or provide an example of what you did during that day when you worked from home."

Let's be clear, Chris Bayliss and Ross Smith didn't do anything *really* radical. It is the boss' job, after all, to look for ways of improving the way work gets done in their organization and to create a culture that fits with their personal style of operating. But for every one of these stories, I can point to 10 stories of bosses who chose *not* to challenge the management systems they inherited. These more conventional bosses chose to prioritize other things, and perhaps they lacked the creativity or tolerance of uncertainty that Bayliss and Smith exhibited.

So of course I strongly encourage you, as a boss, to challenge how work gets done in your part of the organization. This doesn't mean taking inordinate levels of risk. We sometimes hear about case studies of truly radical approaches to management – Ricardo Semler at Semco, Lars Kolind at Oticon – but there are enough examples of better ways of working out there, from books such as this one, for your approach to be both progressive and proven at the same time.

But what if you are not the boss? If you are a mid-level person within a sizeable organization and you are getting frustrated by the sclerotic management processes getting in your way, do you have any possibility of making changes? Well the answer is yes, but you need to proceed cautiously and to take very seriously the notion of experimentation.

Bureaucracy-busting at Roche. Consider this example from the Swiss pharmaceutical giant, Roche. The company has a mission that puts innovation at the heart of what it does, but among many employees the perception is that bureaucracy detracts from this mission. So in 2009 a cross-functional team, working under the banner of a leadership development program, set about trying to shake things up. Realizing that they couldn't tackle bureaucracy as a whole, they decided to focus on one particular process, travel and expense claims. That might not seem the sexiest call, but it had several advantages. After all, the team wanted to test a general hypothesis – that cutting bureaucracy was not only feasible but desir-able – and travel expenses ticked all the criteria. It certainly epitomized in fairly extreme form the misalignment of values that drains profes-sional effort and commitment. "I'm responsible for $60m sales but need approval to buy a $3 cup of coffee," as one participant manager summed up the general mood. As well, the team was startled to find that Roche Pharma's annual travel budget added up to more than $300m – so the stakes were potentially higher than many people had expected[8].

To make progress, the team planned and got permission for an experiment. They came up with an ingenious design comprising two pairs of matched groups, one pair taken from the Basel headquarters, the other from a sales affiliate in Germany. In each pair there were 50 people per group, so a sample of 200 people in all. One group was a control whose travel authorization process continued to operate as before – those "participants" had no change in their current process. The second group in each location, however, was told that as part of the pilot project their travel was to become self-authorized. Subject, of course, to normal company policy (who was entitled to travel business class, etc.), Roche employees made the decision to travel and book their flights and hotels, with no further approvals (no approval to travel and no signature for expenses after the trip). The proviso was that expenses information would be transparent, posted on the Intranet for other employees to see.

The experiment was designed to test three things. Would people be more motivated by removal of the bureaucratic process of pre-authorization? Was the new process simpler than before? And what would be the consequences for costs? The first two were measured by before-and-after surveys. To avoid as far as possible the operation of a "Hawthorne effect" (people working harder and better because they know they are being watched) the team had taken care to downplay the experimental nature of the project by keeping it very low key.

The results were astonishing. Instead of the neutral to modest improvement expected, 45% of participants said motivation had increased as a result of the changes, with another 46% reporting no change; 83% of the sample felt that the approach was better attuned with Roche values and wanted it adopted as normal procedure. Only a very small minority – 6% – were uncomfortable with having their expenses available for others to see. Similarly overwhelming majorities (74% and 87%) reported that the new process was more efficient and took less time than the old one – "Inefficient approval process for travel; sometimes I have the feeling I work at a government authority," was one heartfelt comment. As to cost, the team had fully expected travel costs to go up with self-authorization. In actual fact, the expenses of the two experimental groups went down, one quite substantially, while totals of the two control groups were unchanged. This was something of a revelation. "I hope my expenses will motivate others to spend as little as I do!"

The experiment was a real eye-opener for the members of the team. The idea that "insight" into travel expenditure could be more effective than formal "oversight" began to get real attention. In late 2009 they presented their findings to the Executive Committee, and they were asked to put together a roll-out plan to implement it to key sites globally. Their experiment also inspired others in Roche to take a closer look at some of their other management processes, to see where further improvements could be made.

So what are the lessons from the Roche experiment? How might you set about challenging the way your organization works?

Make your hypothesis clear and practical. Everyone has a view on what's wrong in their organization, but typically these ideas are too abstract to act on: there's too much red tape; there is a blame culture; decision-making is too hierarchical. The trick, in designing an experiment, is to move from the abstract to the specific and to strip the problem down to a single statement: A leads to B. For the Roche team, saying that "the company is bureaucratic" was an empty statement. So they focused down on a single process – expense claims processing – and they identified an alternative to the bureaucratic process: peer review. This allowed them to formulate a simple hypothesis: by switching to peer review, rather than formal sign-off, the expense claim system will become more effective.

Move quickly, in small steps. When launching a new project, many people put together a steering committee as a way of getting buy-in and advice from different parts of the organization. This works well for certain types of politically sensitive projects, but it is disastrous for management experiments. The basic logic of experimentation is to try something quickly, with the minimum levels of permission necessary, get feedback, and move on. For the Roche team, the entire experiment was planned and executed within six months. To do this, they chose locations for the experiment where they could get buy-in quickly and they used an off-the-shelf software product for the "peer review" system for

123

monitoring expense claims. Their short timeline also required adjustments to the design in a few places: for example, labour laws in Germany meant that detailed information about expense claims on the peer review system had to be anonymized.

Another example of the value of moving quickly comes from a team of executives I worked with in Scandinavian insurer, If[9]. They were looking to dramatically simplify and improve the quality of their online offering with private insurance customers. Rather than go through the standard development methodology, they got permission to do a six-week experiment. While this created enormous pressure, it was also a key factor in their success: "It focused us and meant we had to cut away all those project management methodologies that add to the time of making change happen," says Katarina Mohlin, a member of the team. "We had to identify shortcuts, like using existing usability studies, rather than setting up a brand new focus group." By positioning it as an experiment, not a pilot, they overcame concerns about whether it would be a success or not. "A pilot requires a detailed business case with cost rationalization. An experiment allows the business case to be developed *after* the initial feasibility has been done," notes Jorgen Hiden, another team member.

Run the new in parallel with the old. Experimentation is inherently risk-averse: it seeks to find a better way forward, while not closing down the option of retreating to the old model. The Roche team recognized the potential for their peer-review based expense-claim system to backfire, so they ran it in parallel with the existing model for the test period. As well as mitigating the risk they were taking, this approach also gave the experiment some much-needed precision. Every pharmaceutical company manager knows that drug testing requires two groups – a treatment group who get the real drug and a control group who get a placebo. By comparing the behavior of the employees under the two different expense-claim systems, the Roche team were simply recreating the experimental model they were familiar with.

Maximize opportunities for learning. It is often said that in order to understand something, you have to try to change it. A well-designed experiment sheds light on how things really work, regardless of the specific outcome, and it usually opens up new avenues that weren't apparent before. For the Roche team, the results of their experiment were clear enough, but they immediately raised additional questions: Why did the test groups spend *less* on travel, when they had additional discretion? What was it about this experiment that had such a positive impact on their engagement level? And what is stopping us – really – from rolling this out across the company?

Notice that implementing an experiment involves a very different mindset to running a pilot, which assumes a particular course of action but with a bail-out clause if things don't go to plan. The guiding philosophy here is to maximize learning, not minimize risk.

MAKING YOUR EXPERIMENTS STICK

I spend a lot of my time working with managers on small-scale experiments of this sort. While they usually yield interesting and valuable findings, the reality is that most of them don't end up getting rolled out company-wide. For example, the expense-claim experiment at Roche was very well received internally, but at the time of writing it had not been implemented across the organization.

So I am often asked, doesn't this frustrate you? And doesn't it call into question the entire logic of experimentation? My answer has three parts.

First, management experiments that challenge the rules serve the important function of forestalling further bureaucratic creep. In my mind, bureaucracy is akin to a gravitational force, and the larger the organization, the stronger the force becomes. This means that large companies have to run as fast as they can just to stand still. They need managers throughout the system to be on their guard; questioning the way things are working, trying out alternatives, and pushing back on new rules and regulations.

Second, the discipline of designing and running a management experiment provides enormous personal learning. These experiments are often run under the auspices of a corporate leadership development program, and one of the key themes in such programs is typically closing the knowing–doing gap. It is useful to talk about this gap, to make people aware of it, but it is even more useful to do something about bridging it. Experimentation provides the bridge: it compels the managers involved to translate their abstract ideas into operational hypotheses and then into a series of discrete actions. These actions can then be scrutinized and evaluated against the original hypothesis. In my experience, this is a really effective way of enhancing the attentiveness and self-awareness of managers.

Third, management experiments are sometimes really successful. For example, the If insurance experiment that was discussed at the beginning of Chapter 5 led directly to a rethinking of the company's entire approach to coaching and mentoring. The experiments conducted by Chris Bayliss and Ross Smith above have both had an enduring impact on their organizations. Many other companies have also had good experiences with their management experiments. The best single source for reading up on these is the Management Innovation Exchange (MIX), a free online resource at www.management exchange.org.

Of course, it should be no surprise that many management experiments don't seem to go anywhere. The essence of innovation in all walks of life is that most ideas fail. A pharmaceutical company needs to screen thousands of potential targets to identify dozens of candidate drugs, in order to yield a single viable new drug. Perhaps the ratios are a bit different in the field of management, but the principle that "failure" is a more likely outcome than "success" is one that we need to continuously remind ourselves of.

MAKING THE BEST OF AN IMPERFECT WORLD

It is very easy to become frustrated by the apparent irrationality of the organizations in which we work. Some people yearn for more rules and procedures as a way of creating order and reducing the amount of time resolving disagreements. However, the more rules and procedures you create, the more depersonalized work becomes and the more introspective and self-defensive people become. To paraphrase Winston Churchill, bureaucracy is the worst organizing model in the world, except for all the others.

So what is the way forward? We can certainly try to identify alternative ways of coordinating our business activities, whether by using more market-like techniques or community-based principles of self-organizing. My previous book, *Reinventing Management*, had an entire chapter on this subject, but for the most part, we will all end up working for large organizations that operate in an imperfect way. Our job, as effective managers, is to develop the tactics and skills to function effectively in such a system.

— 7 —

THE FUTURE OF MANAGEMENT?

My purpose in writing this book has been, simply, to help you become a better boss. By understanding the way your employees think, your own biases and frailties, and the inherent limitations of the organizations in which you work, you should be better positioned to develop strategies and tactics to help your employees do their best work and to get things done yourself. My guidance throughout has been pragmatic – based on a view of how the business world works today, rather than how it might work in a theoretical or idealized world.

This final chapter takes a slightly different approach, by considering how the world of work might change in the years ahead and whether these changes make your job as a manager easier or harder. We all know there are important technological, social, economic, and political changes afoot, and it is important to develop a point of view on what their consequences are likely to be for the type of work we do as managers.

FORCES THAT SHAPE OUR CHOICE OF MANAGEMENT MODEL

It is useful to have a framework for discussing the way management is changing. Here is one way of looking at it, building on my prior book, *Reinventing Management*.

The work of management can be broken down into four dimensions: how we coordinate activities, how we make decisions, how we set objectives, and how we motivate employees. The first two are the "means" by which we get things done and the latter two are "ends" for the organization and for individuals respectively. For each of these dimensions, we can identify a traditional set of management principles that have their roots in the model of management that was developed during the industrial revolution: coordination was achieved through bureaucratic rules and procedures, decisions were made through hierarchical control, objectives were set through alignment around the needs of owners, and motivation was focused on extrinsic factors, principally money.

We can also identify a set of alternative management principles that have emerged over the last few decades: coordination can be achieved through emergence or self-organization, decisions can be made through collective wisdom, objectives can be set through the principle of obliquity (i.e., by aiming at one target, you often hit another one), and motivation can be based on intrinsic factors, such as achievement, recognition, or self-actualization.

The key idea with this framework is that a company can define its own management model, based around its chosen positions on each of the four dimensions. While many large, traditional companies gravitate to the left side of the framework (see Figure 7.1) and many newer and smaller companies gravitate to the right side, there is nothing inherently right or wrong about these choices. Rather, the position your company takes should reflect its chosen position in the market and the beliefs of the people running the company about its distinctive value proposition.

I often use this framework in seminars with executives and I take them through the following exercise. I ask them, first, to plot how they would position their company today on each of the four dimensions. Then I ask them to plot where they would like to see their company positioned five years from now. Figure 7.1 shows the average scores I have received for this exercise.

Unsurprisingly, the vast majority of respondents position their "wanted" position five years from now to the right of their "current"

Figure 7.1   Management Model Framework

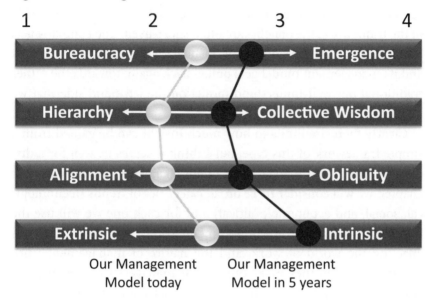

position, and typically by quite a long way – a whole point on a four-point scale. I then ask them, if we went back and asked the same questions again five years from now, where would their companies *actually* be positioned? Almost without fail, people say they would be "stuck" on the white dots, that is, in the same place as they are today. Of course, I cannot prove this is true, but it is remarkable how consistent and widespread the view that there is unlikely to be very much change.

So what is going on here? After a spirited debate about the factors that are preventing their companies from changing, most groups come around to the following view. There are, in essence, powerful forces pulling in both directions, that is, to the left (inertia) and to the right (change). But they are rather different types of forces. The forces pulling to the left are things that managers have little control over – external regulation, a weak economy, labor unions, the overall size and age of the company, and so on. The forces pulling to the right include the potential offered by social and technological change, and also the courage and leadership skills of the people running the company. In essence, these forces tend to cancel each other out over time. While companies frequently try new things, and sometimes succeed in pushing their management model towards the right side of the framework, the benefits are often short-lived. The company gets into trouble, or a recession looms, or new regulations are brought in, and its management model gets pulled back again, towards the rather traditional but well-understood model on the left-hand side that we all recognize.

Clearly there are limits to how much insight can be gained from a simple framework of this type, but I think it serves us well for a discussion of the ways management might change in the future. In this chapter, we will consider three broad categories of trends (technological, social, and economic/political) and for each one we will use the framework to discuss some important questions: How are these trends affecting the world of work, and the nature of management work in particular? Do they make our jobs as managers easier or harder? And do they require us to change our skillsets, our attitudes, and our behaviors?

TECHNOLOGICAL CHANGE: WEB 2.0

The twin engines of technological change – processing power and connectivity – are continuing to revolutionize many aspects of our working lives. Using my management model framework (Figure 7.1), technology is clearly making it possible for coordination of activities to take place through less bureaucratic methods, and for decisions to be made with much greater involvement and input from people across the organization.

Many commentators use the term Web 2.0 as a shorthand for an important qualitative shift in how technology is influencing work. If the first generation of the Internet (Web 1.0) was a one-way flow of information on to your laptop computer, the second generation (Web 2.0) is a two-way conversation in which you, the user, are also a contributor. For example, if you have ever posted a review on Amazon, or commented on a blog, or provided a vote, link, or tag on something you have read, then you have contributed to the organic, fast-evolving world of Web 2.0. The Internet is no longer a vehicle for transmitting information to a large audience; it is now a medium for sophisticated forms of interaction and exchange. Open source software organizations such as Linux and Apache, for example, have succeeded in creating high-quality software products, as good as anything Microsoft or Google has to offer, through the voluntary coordinated efforts of thousands of people who have never met.

So it goes without saying that Web 2.0 is enabling more effective lateral coordination between people and is contributing to a more bottom-up approach to decision-making. But my focus in this book is much narrower: I want to know if these technological advances are changing the nature of work that you do, as a manager of others.

Let's consider a specific example. Most business people today have tried microblogging sites such as Yammer (now owned by Microsoft), which seek to bring the free-flowing style of interaction offered by Facebook to the corporate world. These are password protected sites where people in the same company will share views on topics of interest, but they are hosted externally, so they don't get suffocated by the rules and standards that Corporate Intranets often impose.

The IT services company, CapGemini, is a very active user of Yammer[1]. Its former CTO, Andy Mulholland, describes it as a means of decentralizing the information flow at CapGemini to create greater collaboration from the outside in. The consultants "at the edge" use it as a way of posing questions and sharing their insights, and because they encounter new challenges and opportunities before those at the center, it becomes a useful knowledge-sharing tool. In addition, the company has experimented with "YamJams," webcasts where Yammer works as a back channel for people to hold conversations while the executive concerned is presenting or to send comments in real time. The CEO is known to regularly go on to Yammer and check out who the top thread followers and creators are and what they're discussing.

Problem-solving is also a major area of usage, with people asking for support or help in tracking down a colleague or information resource. One thread starts with the request: "We need more Level 3 and 4 Certified Software Engineers." Other threads revolve around building communities of interest on a particular topic, such as "We are working on Technovision 2011 (a thought leadership publication). What Technology trends should we absolutely not forget to include?"

There are three groups of users. The hugely active group comprises around 50 people who are managing communities and ensuring that Yammer is working all the time. There are around 300 regular Yammer users, and then there are the thousands of "listeners," those users who perhaps use Yammer for a specific purpose, to follow a thread about a topic that resonates with them[2].

So how does microblogging change the work of management? CapGemini uses Yammer for aligning activities, problem-solving, information-sharing, and providing clarification. Now think about the things you do for a living as a manager – and you quickly end up with a pretty similar list. Yammer and related technologies are increasingly being used to provide the support and input that employees used to get from their managers.

This frees up managers, in turn, to spend more time on the real value-added work – such as motivating their employees, structuring their work to make it more engaging, developing their skills, securing access to resources, and making linkages to other parts of the organization. It wouldn't be stretching the point too far to note that all the key things we ought to do as managers "to enable our employees to do their best work" are still required in the world of Web 2.0, whereas all the things we used to do, because they helped us to retain control, are now done quicker and more effectively through technology.

Of course, we have heard parts of this argument before. The original boom in IT usage in the corporate sector, some 30 years ago, led to predictions of the demise of the middle manager, because the technology would enable senior executives to communicate seamlessly with their front-line managers. Today's new technologies are partly just pushing these trends further forward, but they are also encouraging a much greater amount of interactivity in corporate communication than was possible before, making the information flow richer and more readily interpreted.

The bottom line is that *technological change is clarifying our role as managers*. Warren Buffett is famous for saying that it is only when the tide goes out that you can see who is swimming naked, and the same metaphor applies here. When employees can get all the basic support they need for their work through microblogging sites, rather than through their line manager, the real qualities of the line manager are exposed.

SOCIAL CHANGES: GENERATION Y AND TRANSPARENCY

There are many social changes underway that are shaping the business world: the ageing population, a greater focus on health and well-being, awareness of sustainability issues, female empowerment, a greater emphasis on transparency in society, and so on. Again, the focus here is not on the way these trends are shaping business as a whole. Rather, I am interested in how, if at all, social changes are influencing the nature of managerial work. I suggest two are particularly relevant in this regard.

First, is the emergence *of Generation Y*, those people born after 1980 who are now entering the workforce in significant numbers. It is frequently argued that these individuals bring with them a different set of expectations about work and a different set of skills, in comparison to Generation X and the Baby Boomers. For example, it is suggested that they want freedom in everything they do; they love to customize and personalize; they are the collaboration and relationship generation; they have a need for speed[3]. It is open to debate whether these are life-stage, rather than generational, differences, but even the most skeptical observers recognize that Generation Y is far more technology-savvy and able to multitask than Baby Boomers like myself. Here is one data point: one study showed the Generation Y employees who were *more* committed to the companies they were working for were also the ones who were spending *more* time online using Facebook and other social networking sites during their working hours[4]. Far from being a distraction, Facebook usage was seen by these employees as an integral part of their *modus operandi* at work.

How does our work as managers change when our team is mostly made up of Generation Y employees? The "good news" is that these employees were brought up in an era of prosperity and safety, and they have no memory of the period of industrial strife that many Baby Boomers experienced in the 1960s and 1970s. Recall the stories I recounted in Chapter 3 about intransigent and cynical workers – those were stories from the Baby Boomer generation, and they would not resonate at all with a typical Generation Y worker.

The "bad news," on the other hand, is that Generation Y employees are more tolerant of uncertainty. They are less likely to put up with a dull job or a bad boss, because societal norms have moved away from the notion of a job for life, and because the marketplace for jobs is more efficient than it has ever been. Turnover rates are on the rise: in the fast-food sector, it is often greater than 100% per year, and rates of 30–50% per year in other fast growing sectors, such as IT services, are not uncommon.

Again, the net effect of this trend is that your qualities as a manager are more exposed than ever before. I don't believe Generation Y employees are any more or less ambitious than previous generations, but they are more willing, and more able, to change jobs when things aren't going their way. To the extent that you, as their boss, want to get the best out of them, you need to be more thoughtful about the type of work you give them and the conditions in which they are expected to do it.

The other social trend to consider here is the dramatic increase in *transparency*, at all levels. From geopolitical issues (the Arab Spring, Wikileaks) to business scandals (phone hacking at News International, fraudulent accounting at Olympus) to debates on corporate values (Google, Facebook), the common theme is that nothing is truly secret any more. Technological advances make it much easier to gather, assimilate, and distribute information than before and society increasingly accepts that higher levels of openness and transparency are OK. Of course, this shift is not happening without debate, and indeed many people are worried about how much Google or Facebook know about us, but the broad trend here is taking us in one direction only, namely towards greater transparency. People are asking institutions of all types, from government to church to corporations, to be more open about their actions, and to take greater responsibility for the consequences of those actions.

The point here is that social change is legitimizing the increasing transparency that is underway in the business world. On many dimensions of management, companies are becoming more open in their activities. For example:

- Software companies like Red Hat and Atlassian have "open strategy" processes where all employees are invited to contribute to the development of the company's strategic priorities.

- The IT services company, HCL Technologies, has an "open" 360-feedback process, where a manager's feedback from those around him or her is posted online for everyone to review.

- The UK consultancy, Nixon McInnes, has open salaries: everyone knows what everyone else earns and the salary review process starts with the employee proposing how much more he or she should make next year.

These sorts of initiatives have important and fairly predictable consequences for how managers conduct themselves. Greater transparency means that you as a manager can no longer hide behind a wall of "privileged" information. You have to become more tolerant of feedback and you have to become better at influencing others through the quality of your arguments. It is harder work, and typically takes longer, but the potential for higher-quality outputs is greater.

ECONOMIC AND POLITICAL CHANGES: THE SHIFT FROM WEST TO EAST

It goes without saying that economic and political changes are creating new challenges for corporate executives. At the time of writing this book, the big stories were political uncertainty and economic stagnation in Europe, a likely slowdown in growth in China, fiscal uncertainty in the United States, and continuing unrest in the Middle East. With all such trends, there are first-order consequences for business, in terms of demand, regulation, taxation, labor, and so on. My interest here is on the second- and third-order consequences of these changes, in terms of how shifts in the economic and political landscape will affect how companies and individuals operate.

One obvious set of consequences is that managers will need to develop new capabilities. They will have to become better at operating in a "virtual" manner, that is, coordinating teams across multiple time zones and overseeing employees whom they rarely meet face to face. They will also have to figure out how to manage businesses growing at very different rates in different parts of the world. Emotional intelligence, especially in terms of sensitivity to different national cultures, will be more important than ever.

However, there is something deeper going on here as well. If we buy the argument that the center of gravity of the business world is shifting from "West" (North America and Europe) to "East" (Asia), then it is worth considering if we are on the cusp of important parallel changes in the way we think about management[5].

Consider how US hegemony – in all respects – is fading. In the years following the Second World War, it dominated the global business world, as the major source of capital, the home of advanced manufacturing, and the source of most major technological developments. It provided the best-quality management education and it was the source of all the latest management thinking.

In today's more complex, plural world, the biggest sources of capital are the large Sovereign Wealth Funds of the Middle East, Russia, and China. Leadership in advanced manufacturing is spread across such countries as Japan, Korea, Germany, and the US. Technological innovation is dispersed across the world. Top-quality business schools exist in every major market. In short, the rest of the world has caught up. North America no longer holds a clear advantage in any of these fields of accomplishment, but with one exception: management ideology.

By management ideology, I mean the basic assumptions we use to talk about the practice and profession of management. The "traditional" management ideology I described above was largely developed by academics based in the US, studying US companies, with a few notable exceptions (e.g., Henri Fayol, Max Weber). Even today, the US hegemony in management ideology endures. The vast majority of faculty at the top business schools in Europe and Asia gained their PhDs in North America. The top management journals, from *Fortune* to *Harvard Business Review*, are all based in North America. The top management consultancies, from McKinsey to BCG, Bain, and Booz Allen, all have deep American roots.

One consequence of this dominance is that other perspectives get suppressed. There are strong traditions of management writing in both the French and German languages, but they are being marginalized: the up-and-coming scholars in Continental Europe are increasingly writing for English-language journals, and large French and German companies are increasingly bringing in North American trained consultants and academics to advise them. As for the developing world, there is no better way of proving that you are an ambitious, progressive company, than by hiring "professional" managers and advisors that cut their teeth in the North American system: look at Ambev (Brazil), Infosys (India), Huawei (China), DTEK (Ukraine), or Korea Telecom. The entire business world is seemingly in thrall to the dominant American ideology of management. America may have lost its lead in other areas of business, but it still holds sway in this one, vital area.

So should we expect to see a shift in management ideology away from North America and towards Asia? And if yes, what will it look like?

My view is that such a shift is highly likely, but will take many years to transpire. Using the current measures of what constitutes effective management, the American model is better than what is on offer in other countries[6], and at the moment companies in the emerging "BRIC" economies are simply trying to catch up. However, there is no reason to believe that this state of affairs will last forever. Many observers have commented on America's declining influence over the world, and the apparently inexorable rise of China and India. As these other countries come to influence the world of business more generally, we should expect them to also influence the way we think about – and implement – the practice of management.

What might an alternative model of management, built on Asian values and capabilities, look like? One starting point is to think about the differences in national culture across regions. For example, the Anglo-American world is relatively individualistic and it has a relatively short-term orientation. Most Asian countries, in contrast, have a more collective orientation and a relatively long-term orientation. So building on these differences, here are a few thoughts about how management might evolve:

- In terms of objective-setting, why don't we put a greater focus on higher-order purpose or vision, rather than short-term financial returns? And what about giving equal emphasis to multiple stakeholders, rather than focusing singularly on shareholders?

- In terms of coordination, can we imagine putting a greater focus on self-organization and collective wisdom, rather than bureaucratic rules and procedures, as a way of getting things done?

- In terms of outcomes, should we put a greater emphasis on innovation, creativity, and employee engagement, rather than just productivity and efficiency?

These are questions not statements. We know more about the limitations of our existing model than what the alternative would look like, but there is some evidence that these alternative approaches are starting to take hold. For example, a recent book, *The India Way*, sought to identify the distinctive characteristics of the most successful Indian companies, and it focused on "holistic engagement with employees," "improvisation and adaptability," and "broad mission and purpose." These features, the authors claimed, were inspired partly from ancient writings, such as the *Bhagavad Gita*, and partly from the experience Indian executives had growing up in the chaotic post-war years[7]. We can imagine similar books being written on the *China Way* or the *Brazilian Way* in the years ahead.

In sum, there are good reasons to expect the dominant model of management to evolve as regions of the world, other than the US, move into the ascendancy. Think back to Figure 7.1 earlier in the chapter: the management principles on the left side, especially those concerned with extrinsic rewards and alignment of objectives, are much more consistent with Anglo-American cultural values than those on the right side. If we expect to see a shift towards greater emphasis on collectivity and long-term orientation, then the right side of the framework becomes a more logical and desirable place to sit.

CONCLUSION: MAKING THE RIGHT CHOICES

This brief discussion of trends suggests a consistent theme: the practice of management is becoming both more challenging and more rewarding. Technology is making many of the traditional aspects of management redundant, freeing up our time to do the more value-added parts of our work. Social change is making employees more demanding. Political and economic shifts are exposing us to different models of management that are more long-term oriented and less shareholder-focused.

Using the framework I introduced earlier, we can expect the management model in large organizations to move gradually away from the traditional one based on bureaucracy, hierarchy, extrinsic rewards, and alignment. Gradually is the key word here: the inertial forces pulling us back towards the world we know, and are comfortable with, are strong. But it seems inevitable that organizations will gradually align themselves to the demands placed on them and the opportunities they face.

Managing well is about developing greater awareness of what our employees need, where our own biases and limitations lie, and how our organizations really function. It is about doing what works, rather than what comes naturally, and this requires a considerable amount of self-discipline and personal development.

However, managing well is also about making explicit choices, and these sometimes involve departing from the tried-and-tested models that others are pursuing. I believe the trends outlined here are taking us in one direction only, with our employees and our broader stakeholders all demanding change. The question to ask ourselves, as individual managers and as agents of change within our own organizations, is whether we want to be the leaders or laggards in this process of evolution. We can seek to improve the nature of management ourselves or we can allow others to do it for us.

ENDNOTES

Introduction

1 Google's Quest to Build a Better Boss, Adam Bryant, *The New York Times*, March 12, 2012.
2 The words in quotations are taken from news articles: see the Financial Services Authority report on the collapse of RBS, www.fsa.gov.uk; the National Commission on the BP Deepwater Horizon Oil Spill and Offshore Drilling, Chief Counsel's Report, Chapter 5; the quote about Rupert Murdoch from www. newscorpwatch.org.

Chapter 1

1 For example: (1) Harter, J.K., Schmidt, F.L., and Hayes, T.L., Business-unit-level relationship between employee satisfaction, employee engagement, and business outcomes: a meta-analysis, *Journal of Applied Psychology*, 2002, 87(2): 268–279; (2) Fulmer, I.S., Gerhart, B., and Scott, K.S., Are the 100 best better? An empirical investigation of the relationship between being a "great place to work" and firm performance, *Personnel Psychology*, 2003, 56(4): 965–993; (3) MacLeod, D. and Clarke, N., *Engaging for Success*, 2009, http://www.bis.gov.uk/files/file52215.pdf.
2 http://www.engageforsuccess.org/.
3 Edmans, A., Does the stock market fully value intangibles? Employee satisfaction and equity prices. *Journal of Financial Economics*, 2011, 101(3): 621–640.
4 Quoted in Edmans, op cit, page 1.
5 See, for example: (1) Nyberg, A., The impact of managerial leadership on stress and health among employees, Doctoral Thesis, Karolinska Institute, Stockholm, 2009, ISBN 978-91-7409-614-9; (2) Gillet, N., Fouquereau, E., Forest, J., Brunault, P., and Colombat, P., The impact of organizational factors on psychological needs and their relations with well-being, *Journal of Business and Psychology*, 2011, DOI: 10.1007/s10869-011-9253-2; (3) Crabtree, S., Engagement keeps the doctor away, *Gallup Management Journal*, 2005.

6 Mol, M. and Birkinshaw, J.M., *Giant Steps in Management*, FT Prentice Hall, London, 2008.

7 Levy, F., The World's Happiest Countries, Forbes.com, July 14, 2010.

8 David Cameron's speech on November 24, 2010, www.number10.gov.uk.

9 Smith, G., Why I am Leaving Goldman Sachs, *New York Times*, March 14, 2012. Smith also published a book on this same topic which came out in late 2012, though it did not create the same level of interest.

10 TUC, What Do Workers Want?, YouGov poll for the TUC, August 2008.

11 CIPD Employee Outlook survey, Spring 2012, www.cipd.co.uk.

12 These data are taken from a current research project by the author.

13 This survey was conducted by myself and Gary Hamel, based on the ideas Gary developed in a *Harvard Business Review* article, Moonshots for Management, February, 2009.

14 Academic evidence for this point is strong. For example: McDuffie, J.P., Human resource bundles and manufacturing performance: organizational logic and flexible production systems in the world auto industry, *Industrial and Labor Relations Review*, 1995, 48(2): 197–221.

Chapter 2

1 Quotes taken from www.huffingtonpost.com, Margaret Heffernan blog, John Browne's BP Memoir: Not So Much Beyond Business as Beyond Belief, June 7, 2010, and from www.guardian.co.uk, Tom Bower, June 2, 2010.

2 Phil Rosenzweig, *The Halo Effect*, Pocket Books, 2008.

3 Walter Isaacson, *Steve Jobs*, Simon & Schuster, 2011, page 124.

4 Fred Goodwin quotes taken from: Hancock, M. and Zahawi, N., *Masters of Nothing*, Biteback Publishing, 2011, page 167, www.ianfraser.org; *The Times*, February 2009. Steve Jobs quotes taken from Isaacson, 2011, op cit. The odd numbered quotes are about Goodwin, the even numbered ones are about Jobs.

5 Isaacson, 2011, op cit, page 112.

6 The colleagues who helped me here were Lisa Duke, Stefano Turconi, and Vyla Rollins.

7 The Krauthammer Observatory: Time for the yearly performance review . . . of our managers! *Steffi Gande*, Issue 4, 2010, www.krauthammer.com.

Chapter 3

1 Ezzamel, M., Wilmott, H., and Worthington, F., Power, control and resistance in "the factory that time forgot," *Journal of Management Studies*, 2001, 38(8): 1053–1079.

2 Unfortunately, the story of Northern Plant does not have a neat and tidy conclusion. Mike did not sack all the recalcitrant workers, nor did he win them all over. He and his colleagues continued to push the new management practices and workers continued to find ways of pushing back. The researchers concluded that "notwithstanding the changes in the technical organization of production that occurred, there had been little substantive change in the social organization of production."

3 Ezzamel, M. and Wilmott, H., Accounting for teamwork: a critical study of group-based systems of organizational control, *Administrative Science Quarterly*, 1998, 43: 358–396. Also see: Jenkins, S. and Delbridge, R., Disconnected workplaces: interests and identities in the "High Performance Factory," in *Searching for the H in HRM* (eds S. Bolton and M. Houlihan), Palgrave Macmillan, Basingstoke, 2007.

4 See, for example: Ryan, R.M. and Deci, E.L., Self-determination theory and the facilitation of intrinsic motivation, social development, and well-being, *American Psychologist*, 2000, 55(1): 68–87; MacGregor, D., *The Human Side of Enterprise*, Irwin/McGraw-Hill, New York, 1960; Herzberg, F., *The Motivation to Work*, John Wiley & Sons, Inc., New York, 1959. For a more practical slant on these topics, see Pink, D., *Drive*, Riverhead Books, New York, 2009.

5 This point is developed in a detailed academic study: Gruenberg, B., The Happy Worker: an analysis of educational and occupational differences in determinants of job satisfaction, *American Journal of Sociology*, 1980, 86(2): 247–270.

6 These data were taken from the UK Office of National Statistics. The job satisfaction data come from www.bath.ac.uk/news/pdf/rose-table.pdf. The job pay data come from http://www.ons.gov.uk/ons/rel/ashe/annual-survey-of-hours-and-earnings/ashe-results-2011/ashe-statistical-bulletin-2011.html.

7 Deming, E., *Out of the Crisis*, MIT Press, 1968.

8 For example: Buckingham, M. and Clifton, D., *Now Discover Your Strengths*, Simon & Schuster UK, 2004.

9 Gibson, C., Cooper, C., and Conger, J.A., Do you see what we see? The complex effects of perceptual distance between leaders and teams, *Journal of Applied Psychology*, 2009, 94(1): 62–76.

10 For a practical example of this, see De Botton, A., *The Pleasures and Sorrows of Work*, Hamish Hamilton, 2009.

Chapter 4

1 *Time Magazine*, June 27, 2011, From Dr Oz to Mr Oz, page 34.

2 I recounted this same story in an earlier book, *Reinventing Management*. Apologies to those (few) readers who have actually read both books in their entirety.

3 Taken from Bob Sutton's blog, May 6, 2010, Boos an Empathy: CEO John Lilly on why the best leaders think and act like teachers, Bobsutton.typepad.com.

4 The story is taken from *Imagine: How Creativity Works* by Jonah Lehrer, Canongate Books, 2012.

5 Page 1 of *The Essential Drucker* by Peter Drucker, Taylor & Francis Group, 2007.

6 Author interviews with Anand Pillai.

7 Dan Bean wrote this story on the Management Innovation Exchange website: http://www.managementexchange.com/story/we-org.

8 Julian Birkinshaw blog, Getting the Right People on the Right Projects, http://bsr.london.edu/blog/post-34/index.html.

9 Bernd Schmitt, *Customer Experience Management*, John Wiley & Sons, Ltd, 2003.

10 Author interviews with Shanmugam Nagarajan (Nags). See corporate website: http://247-inc.com.

11 Frederick F. Reichheld, *The Loyalty Effect*, Harvard Business Press, 1996.

12 Julian Birkinshaw, "A True Measure of Leadership," Labnotes Issue 21, www.managementlab.org.

Chapter 5

1 This story was first described in: Birkinshaw, J.M. and Caulkin, S., *Business Strategy Review*, Winter 2012.

2 Kahneman, D., *Thinking Fast and Slow*, Allen Lane, 2011, page 20.

3 Nicholson, N, Evolutionary psychology: toward a new view of human nature and organizational society, *Human Relations*, 2007, 50(9): 1053–1078.

4 This notion of management as an unnatural act has been around for a while. See, for example: Suters, E.T., *The Unnatural Act of Management*, 1992; Boyatzis, R.E., Cowen, S.S., and Kolb, D.A., *Innovation in Professional Education: Steps on a Journey from Teaching to Learning*, Jossey-Bass, 1995, page 50.

5 Hurst, D.A., *The New Ecology of Leadership*, Columbia Business School Press, 2011, page 247.

6 The notion of a signature process was developed by my colleague Lynda Gratton. See: Gratton, L. and Ghoshal, S., Beyond Best Practice, *Sloan Management Review*, 2005, 46(3): 49–57.

7 Ray Dalio's management model has been discussed quite frequently in the media. See, for example: Cassidy, J, Mastering the Machine, *The New Yorker*, July 25, 2011. Dalio's principles can be found at: http://www.bwater.com/Uploads/FileManager/Principles/Bridgewater-Associates-Ray-Dalio-Principles.pdf.

8 This is a research study I am conducting in collaboration with Jordan Cohen at PA Consulting. At the time of writing this book, we had not completed the research.

9 Svenson, O., Are we all less risky and more skillful than our fellow drivers?, *Acta Psychologica*, 1981, 47(2): 143–148; Zuckerman, E.W. and Jost, J.T., What makes

you think you're so popular? Self evaluation maintenance and the subjective side of the "Friendship Paradox," *Social Psychology Quarterly*, 2001, 64(3): 207–223.

10 Tetlock, P.E., *Expert Political Judgement: How Good is it?*, Princeton University Press, 2005.

11 Cooper, A.C., Woo, C.Y. and Dunkelberg, W.C., Entrepreneurs' perceived chances for success, *Journal of Business Venturing*, 1988, 3: 97–108; Astebro, T., Assessing the commercial viability of new ventures, *Canadian Investment Review*, Spring 2003, pages 18–25.

12 Malmendier, U. and Tate, G., Does overconfidence affect corporate investment? CEO overconfidence measures revisited, *European Financial Management*, 2005, 11(5): 649–659.

13 Nicholson, N., Personality and entrepreneurial leadership: a study of the heads of the UK's most successful independent companies, *European Management Journal*, 2008, 16: 529–539.

14 Cassidy, J., Mastering the Machine, *New Yorker Magazine*, July 25, 2011.

15 Harford, T., *Adapt: Why Success Always Starts with Failure*, Abacus Books, 2011.

16 Kahneman, D., op cit, page 55.

17 Vohs, K., The psychological consequences of money, *Science*, 314: 1154–1156.

18 Danziger, S., Levav, J., and Avniam-Pesso, L., Extraneous factors in judicial decisions, *Proceedings of the National Academy of Science*, 2011, 108: 6889–6892.

19 Meehl, P.E., *Clinical versus statistical prediction: a theoretical analysis and a review of the evidence*, University of Minnesota Press, 1954.

20 This paper by Orley Ashenfelter is available at: http://www.terry.uga.edu/economics/docs/ashenfelter_predicting_quality.pdf.

21 Weick, K.M. and Guinote, A., When subjective experiences matter: power increases reliance on the ease of retrieval, *Journal of Personality and Social Psychology*, 2008, 94: 956–970.

22 See, for example: Duhigg, C., *The Power of Habit*, William Heinemann, London, 2012.

23 Karl Weick has written many academic articles on "High Reliability Organisations." The best practical way of getting to grips with his ideas is his book: Weick, K.E. and Sutcliffe, K., *Managing the Unexpected*, John Wiley & Sons, Ltd, 2007.

24 See Ariely, D., *Predictably Irrational*, Harper, 2008. Dan Ariely also has a blog with all his latest ideas, and from which I took this quote: www.danariely.com.

25 Savage, S., Skill, luck and human frailty, GLG Views, from the company's website: www.glgpartners.com.

Chapter 6

1 Marx, K., *Capital: Critique of Political Economy*, 1867.

2 Crozier, M., *The Bureaucratic Phenomenon*, 1964.

3 Hope, J. and Fraser, R., *Beyond Budgeting*, Harvard Business School Press, Boston, 2003.

4 Personal interviews with Jordan Cohen. There is also a case study published by IESE Business School: Jordan Cohen at PfizerWorks: Building the Office of the Future, IESE DPI-187-E, 2009.

5 See: Klein, J., *Hacking Work*, 2009, for some nice examples of risky bottom-up initiatives.

6 This story about Chris Bayliss at Bank of New Zealand is taken from an article written by him in the Management Innovation Exchange. http://www.managementexchange.com/story/not-just-ordinary-day-beach-unshackling-employees-bank-new-zealand.

7 Personal interviews with Ross Smith. Part of this story was also referenced in my previous book, *Reinventing Management*.

8 This story was taken from "Roche: From Oversight to Insight," Labnotes Issue 16, www.managementlab.org.

9 This story was taken from "Giving Customers What They Want," Labnotes Issue 20, www.managementlab.org.

Chapter 7

1 The CapGemini case was written up in "A Common Thread: Microblogging at CapGemini," Labnotes Issue 19, www.managementlab.org.

2 To make sure it is used prudently, CapGemini has developed a code of conduct, which starts: Yammer is "a source of instant inspiration to strengthen and empower its members to face their daily impediments and foster the development of international social networks around common areas of interest.". Importantly, because Yammer is hosted by an independent company, not by a central IT department, no confidential or client-specific matters are discussed.

3 Tapscott, D., *Grown Up Digital*, McGraw-Hill, New York, 2009, page 35.

4 This research was conducted by You at Work, a leading player in the market for flexible benefits consulting (corporate.youatwork.co.uk). It was reported in: Julian Birkinshaw, Play Hard, Work Hard, *People Management*, October 30, 2008, page 46.

5 These ideas were first developed in a blog: http://www.managementexchange.com/users/julian-birkinshaw.

6 See: "Why American Management Rules the World" by Nick Bloom and colleagues, http://blogs.hbr.org/cs/2011/06/why_american_management_rules.html.

7 Capelli, P., Singh, H., Singh, J., and Useem, M., *The India Way*, Harvard Business Press, 2010.

INDEX

149

INDEX

INDEX